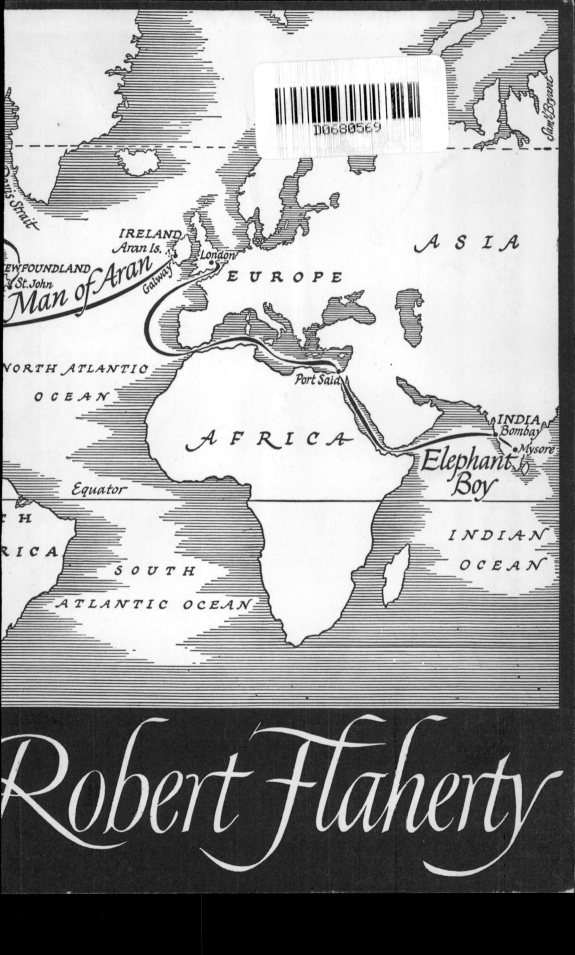

The World of Robert Flaherty

THE WORLD OF

Robert Flaherty

by RICHARD GRIFFITH

with over seventy photographs

DUELL, SLOAN AND PEARCE · NEW YORK

LITTLE, BROWN AND COMPANY · BOSTON

DUELL, SLOAN AND PEARCE — LITTLE, BROWN
BOOKS ARE PUBLISHED BY
LITTLE, BROWN AND COMPANY
IN ASSOCIATION WITH
DUELL, SLOAN & PEARCE, INC.

Published simultaneously
in Canada by McClelland and Stewart Limited

PRINTED IN THE UNITED STATES OF AMERICA

TO IRIS BARRY

who said

"The film is a machine for seeing more than meets the eye."

Acknowledgments

This book largely owes its existence to the initiative of Miss Evelyn Gerstein, who interested the publishers in it, and indefatigably taskmastered the writer to its completion. I owe her a large debt of gratitude. It was begun under the eye of Robert Flaherty, who read the bulk of it before his death in 1951. Since then, I have had the constant help and advice of Frances Hubbard Flaherty and David Flaherty, who also opened to me a vast treasure house of diaries, letters, still-photographs, and other memorabilia. To Mrs. Flaherty I owe especial thanks for her editorial judgment and her fine ear for words.

Excerpts from Robert Flaherty's books, *My Eskimo Friends* and *The Captain's Chair,* and from Frances Hubbard Flaherty's *Elephant Dance* are used by kind permission of the Flahertys and of Charles Scribner's Sons. Pat Mullen and E. P. Dutton and Company have permitted me to use passages from Mr. Mullen's book, *Man of Aran.*

I have also to thank Mrs. Oscar Godbout for many services; and my wife, Ann Warren Griffith, for unfailing enthusiasm for the book and its subject.

R. G.

With the exception of the final photograph by Pousset-d'Art, to whom special acknowledgment is due, all photographs are from The Robert Flaherty Collection of The Museum of Modern Art Film Library donated to the Museum by Mrs. Robert Flaherty.

"The arts hold immediate communication with nature, and are only derived from that source."

HAZLITT

Contents

Preface

Robert Flaherty, who died July 23, 1951, is known in film history as "the father of the documentary film" — the creator of a method of film-making which takes its themes, its actors, and its settings from life itself. Some of us believe that his method was the first appropriate use of the motion-picture camera, the beginnings of a new narrative art which has not even yet fully come into being. And I for one am certain that if any films of our time survive a century from now, they will be these epics of the spirit of man — *Nanook of the North, Moana, Man of Aran, Elephant Boy, Louisiana Story*, and the others. They are classic because they deal with eternal things.

But this is not a book about Robert Flaherty's contributions to the motion picture, or even about his films as such. It is about the stuff of which the films were made — which in his case was the great globe itself. You might say that for him a film was just an excuse to go adventuring in a new place in the world, to find out what it was like there, and to bring back a fragment of what he found, for the stay-at-homes to look at and delight in.

Many have done much the same thing. Many have taken movie cameras with them in their globe-trottings. The results have often been pretty, and have sometimes been anthropology. If Robert Flaherty's films added to these qualities the extra dimension of drama, it was perhaps because he did not wander at random. He was looking for something wherever he went, always the same thing.

His was the search for what he called the spirit of man, the true elixir. It is a search which has been almost abandoned in our time; and many, to whom his films are an experience like racial memory, ponder what sent him forth on this alchemical quest in a day when science, or some of her voices, say there is no spirit to be found, but only a handful of dust. Once when someone asked him, as someone was always asking him, why he spent so much of his force in filming the primeval, Flaherty looked out and answered: "You forget, I grew up with primitive people, Indians and Eskimos. I was thirty before I knew much about what you call civilization. Maybe I don't know it even now." He came to know it, better than most, but it never effaced what went before. When the young Flaherty saw the towering cliffs of Cape Wolstenholme and the churning seas beneath them, he was seeing the world as it looked before man bent it to his equivocal uses. When he met the Eskimos he was making the acquaintance of our own ancestors, at the time when they first knew they were men and must help each other against the creatures and the elements. If, after that, Robert Flaherty mostly sought the spirit of man in the secret places of the earth, we will not say that that is because there alone does it any more exist. We will say, for our souls' sake, that that was where he best knew how to find it.

Such a search as his comes out of temperament and character, and out of the kind of boyhood which will presently be described. It found its first object when he came to know a people — the people whom we unconsciously insult in calling them Eskimos, for this is the Indian's sneering description of them as "eaters of raw meat." Eaters, devourers, of raw meat they are, but Flaherty came to think of them by the name they call themselves: the Innuit, which means "we, the people." We, the people. For the Eskimos of those days thought that they were the only people there were, to them the desolation they lived in was the entire planet, and their few thousands its whole population. The *kablunak*, the white man, was in his few appearances among them a man from Mars; and the Indian, the Adelite, their nearest neighbor, was also a creature so different as to be almost another species — an inimical species. The Indians got firearms before the Eskimos did and, in the fierce wars that followed, the Innuit learned to fear the Adelite far more than Nanook the Bear, Ivuik the Walrus, or those more bitter enemies, hunger and cold. In that harsh country, depending on them for companionship and daily bread, Flaherty found in the Eskimos a humanity so golden that he carried it with him ever afterwards as a touchstone of judgment. To him, the Eskimos were we the people, as we should be.

Whenever he later wandered, he looked for that same spirit. This is the story of his search, told as far as possible in his own words and pictures, in those of his wife and collaborator, Frances Hubbard Flaherty, and of several companions of the journeys. I have tried to let them speak for themselves, less as the history of a career than as direct experiences of a kind which come to few of us, whether we travel or stay at home. To the lovers of his films, I hope they will bring something of the aftertaste of an old joy, and something of the quality of a life led with greater distinction than any I have known.

RICHARD GRIFFITH

New York, 1952

Introduction

Robert Flaherty was born February 16, 1884, in Iron Mountain, Michigan, the eldest of the seven children of Robert Henry and Susan Kloeckner Flaherty. His grandfather had come from Ireland via Quebec about the middle of the last century, and afterward a great boiling of Flahertys spread across southern Canada and the northern United States. Iron and copper were being taken out of Minnesota and Michigan at a great rate in those days, fortunes were being made, and Flaherty's father turned to mining. But the panic of 1893, which swept across America, laid a heavy hand on Robert, Jr. and his family.

> I remember one incident of that disaster as if it happened yesterday [wrote Flaherty]. For months the mine in which my father had his all-in-all had been closed down. The miners were starving. One day they banded together hundreds strong and marched toward the office where my father was. I watched them gathering round it. Some bombarded the little building with stones; others with axes began chopping the verandah, until suddenly a throng rushed in and began tearing it away. The sound of splintering wood always brings back that terrifying day.
>
> Soon afterwards my father left us and struck out for what was then the little-known frontier, the Lake of the Woods country in Canada, where gold had recently been discovered. After a year he came back to the poverty-stricken country in which we lived. If ever there was a happy reunion it was ours, for he brought with him amazing tales of gold, and out of a great bag, like a genii in *The Arabian Nights,* he drew forth pieces of white, pink, and yellow quartz, speckled and strung with yellow gold . . .

But, boy that I was, he brought me something that was still more wonderful — Indian moccasins, real Indian moccasins, he said. I never wore them. I carried them to school. My particular pals, as a great favor, I let smell them — a smell which is like no other in the world — the Indian smell of smoked buckskin. I slept with them under my pillow at night and dreamed of Indians in a land of gold.

When my father went back he took me with him. For a year I lived in the wilderness, the only boy in the camp, my friends the miners and prospectors who explored the wild unknown country around. Occasionally bands of Indians drifted into camp. They brought me moccasins and, once, a bow and arrows. They even let me come into their tepees now and then. Often, long through the nighttime, they held dances — pow-wows. To the throbbing of their tom-toms I used to fall asleep.

The mine thrived. I was packed out to "civilization" — to Upper Canada College — English masters, Eton suits and collars, and English games, Rugby and cricket. All of which to me was even more strange than I, wild and woolly as I was, must have seemed to the other boys, who spent a great deal of time plying me with questions. There was one boy from Australia who boasted a cattleman's whip which, I did concede, he could crack like a rifle. But didn't I have gold nuggets and Indian moccasins? And besides, I knew a few pidgin Indian words, quite enough to make everyone believe that I spoke real Indian.

Chequered were those school years of mine, as they must always be to anyone born with the instincts of a wanderer. By seventeen I broke away from it all and drifted back to the frontier, to the magic land of Indians, unknown lakes, tangled forests, and mysteriously winding streams. My father was at this time carrying out extensive explorations for iron ore. With his engineers and prospectors I grew up on these explorations, whose range East and West was several times the length and breadth of England.

A last attempt at higher education at the Michigan College of Mines brought him back to the United States. The college quickly decided that he lacked the makings of a mineralogist, at least an academic one, and bluntly fired him. But during this short stay in civilization he met the girl who was to become his wife, Frances Hubbard. She was the daughter of Dr. Lucius L. Hubbard of Boston, collector of minerals, stamps, rare books, rare birds, and an infinitude of college degrees. Among his many interests geology predominated; and since in those days Middle-Western mining operations were largely financed from Boston, it was not unnatural that Dr. Hubbard should have become state geologist of Michigan and, after his retirement from that post, the developer of a new range of copper mines in the upper peninsula. Here he settled with his family.

His daughter Frances had had a conventional finishing, including Bryn Mawr and Europe. But her far from conventional father had provided her with a glimpse of quite another kind of life. The first to chart the interior Maine forests (he was the author of *Woods and Lakes of Maine*), Dr. Hubbard had taken his very young daughter on several trips through this last wilderness of the eastern United States, and the experience was indelible. In Michigan, years later, she resumed it. "I used to go off alone every day on my horse," she remembers, "following the faint, overgrown trails of the old logging days. I would pick out on the map one of the tiny lakes or ponds hidden in the woods and set off to find it. Sometimes I got lost, or darkness fell before I could reach home, and I would spend the night in one of the deserted lumber camps that the forests had swallowed up. What I liked best was to wander all night on the shore of the lake in the moonlight. I thought no one cared about these things but me."

Someone did. A young man who came to Sunday dinner stayed for hours talking to her father about the woods and the lake country. Frances Hubbard had never met such a young man before. Untutored, in the way she thought of tutoring, he seemed to know everything about the wilds she wanted to make her own. Their backgrounds, experiences, their very vocabularies, were as different as night from day, but it was his world she wanted. "I thought, when we were married, we would go live in the woods," she said.

Eventually they lived the equivalent of a life in the woods, but not for many years. For her new husband had already begun what he thought was to be his life's work. Even in the early 1900s, southern Canada was just beginning to be developed, and there was plenty of work for a young man who had absorbed a knowledge of mines and mining from his boyhood days. But there was that in Bob Flaherty that drove him to look beyond the horizon. And there, untapped, lay the great north country, for centuries the exclusive preserve of the Hudson's Bay Company, which remained uninterested in anything besides its furs and fishing grounds. But perhaps there was more to be found in this largely unknown desolation than mink and seal and whale. Perhaps the ore-bearing Animikean strata which emerge in the Mesabi and Menominee ranges of the northern United States cropped out again on the eastern shore of Hudson Bay. Flaherty took this idea to Sir William Mackenzie, who with his daring imagination was to Canada what Cecil Rhodes was to Africa. The magnate's interests, though nearly global, had so far failed to embrace the Far North, and, being another beyond-the-horizoner, he decided to let the young man see what he could find out. In 1910, Flaherty set out on the first of what were to be five exploring expeditions to the north, accomplished over a period of six years.

The end-paper map traces the routes of these first five quests for iron and copper ore. In terms of their original aim, they were a crushing disappointment to the hopes of the explorer and his backer. True, much was accomplished by the way. The interior of the vast Ungava peninsula, known only to the Eskimo, was traversed for the first time by a white man. Wintering on the southern shore of Baffinland, Flaherty made the first attempt to chart the shores of Foxe Channel since Luke Foxe passed that way in 1631 searching for the Northwest Passage. More notable than these "firsts" was a "second," the rediscovery of the Belcher Islands. This sizable land mass was sighted by the seventeenth-century explorers of Hudson Bay, but in the intervening centuries the whalers and mail boats somehow missed it and it was removed from the maps, believed to be mythical or of very small extent. Drawn to them by Eskimo tales, Flaherty found the Belchers to be a huge archipelago, the largest of which, named Flaherty Island by the Canadian government, proved to contain a lake, itself as big as the whole area formerly assigned to the "supposed" Belchers on the Admiralty charts. These were signal contributions to the exploration of the North, but they were the sum of the expeditions' achievements. Flaherty found numerous deposits of iron ore and other minerals in Ungava, in Baffinland, and on the Belchers, but in Ungava, Baffinland, and the Belchers they had to remain. To be worth the difficulty and expense of transporting them out through Hudson Straits to England and the United States, the ore deposits would have to be rich indeed, and Flaherty experienced the defeat of hearing his own father pronounce the Belcher ores too lean for commercial purposes. This decision put a period to Sir William Mackenzie's hopes, and in the warbound Canada of 1916, attempts to develop new natural resources were perforce being abandoned. There seemed to be no reason for Robert Flaherty to go into the North again.

There was, though. In the course of looking for minerals, he had discovered a country and a people who fascinated him and drew him back. The record of his discovery is contained in the diaries he kept of his explorations, from 1910 onwards. Tales from these diaries eventually found their way into his travel book, *My Eskimo Friends,* and his novels, *The Captain's Chair* and *White Master,* but these are only fragments of the complete record which may one day reach his admirers. Written in igloos at night, after days full of herculean effort and scarcely credible hardships, at the time they served chiefly to fill the lonesome hours, but they were really Flaherty's first creative work. They were the first outlet for his story-telling urge, and they show that in the years he was writing them he arrived at a new way of looking at the world and a new relation with his fellow man.

The North

ESKIMO, ESKIMOS, *or* ESQUIMAUX (*a corruption of the Abnaki Indian Eskimantic or the Ojibway Ashkimeq, both terms meaning "those who eat raw flesh"; they call themselves "Innuit," "the people"*). *A North* (*American*)

American Indian people inhabiting the arctic coast of America from Greenland to Alaska . . . never far inland, or south of the region where the winter ice allows seals to congregate. Even on hunting expeditions they never travel more than thirty miles from the coast . . . The Eskimos are solely hunters and fishers, and derive most of their food from the sea . . . They are enormous eaters; two will easily dispose of a seal at one sitting . . . A man will lie on his back and allow his wife to feed him with tit-bits of blubber and flesh until he is unable to move.

The Eskimo cannot strictly be called a wandering race. They are nomadic only in so far as they have to move from place to place during the fishing and shooting season, following the game in its migrations. They have, however, no regular property . . . Long habit and the necessities of their life have also compelled those having food to share with those having none — a custom which, with others, has conduced to the stagnant condition of Eskimo society, and to their utter improvidence.

The Eskimo have no chiefs or political and military rulers. Fabricius concisely described them in his day: "Sine deo, domino, reguntur consuetudine." *The government is mainly a family one, though a man distinguished for skill in the chase, and for strength and shrewdness, often has considerable power in the village. No political or social tie is recognized between the villages, though general good-fellowship seems to mark their relations. They never go to war with each other . . .*

Encyclopaedia Britannica, *11th Edition*

I. HUDSON BAY

Robert flaherty made his first journey to the North for Sir William Mackenzie in 1910. At first the new country seemed no more than a glamorous extension of the southern Canada of his boyhood, where men assaulted the wilderness for the wealth it held. On his way toward James Bay he wrote:

Hudson Bay is mysterious country. The grizzled old fur traders and the fur brigades of strange Indians, curiously garbed, with hair shoulder-long, whom we sometimes ran into, seemed to be people of another world. Down the silent, sombrely forested courses of the Little Ground Hog, into the big Mattagami, and on into the smooth, swift, mile-wide mirror of the Moose was only five days' travel, for though the distance was nearly two hundred miles, the rivers were high and flowing strong.

The rugged granites over which the Mattagami breaks, long "saults," smoking falls, and canyon-slots through the hills, give way about halfway down to a vast muskeg plain which extends for the remainder of the river courses to the sea — a great desolate waste, treeless save along the margins of lakes and streams. Unbrokenly level, in Devonian times, as the fossils in the limestone of its underlying formation show, it was the floor of the now distant sea. Through it the Mattagami, a deep groove, loops and winds.

Wide scars of burnt forest, chafing tangles of tree trunks barked and bleached by the weather, alternate with live forests of fir, silver birches, and long-stemmed, sea-green groves of poplars. Huge portions of it, undermined by the icefields of break-up time in spring and by the floods of the high-water season, lay ava-

3

lanched in chaos on the lower slopes. Trunks, branches, and foliage of the wreckage swayed like deadheads at midstream.

There was little wild life. The raucous cries of wheeling gulls, the "quawk, quawk" of wood duck, were infrequent enough to be startling. Even in the forest places the cawing of some "Whisky Johnny" for bits of bannock and bacon rind, and the forlorn cries of "Poor Canada" were the only sounds. Of natives we saw only signs — gaunt tepee frames, sleeping patches of weather-rusted boughs, and here and there poles that, as they inclined upstream or down, pointed out the travellers' direction, or message sticks bearing scrolls of birch bark covered with charcoal writing in the missionary's syllabic Cree.

The Moose begins, impressively large, where the Missanabi from the West and the Mattagami meet. By nightfall it broadened to three miles. The forests of either shore gave way to dreary wastes of muskeg and to spectres of solitary wind-shapen trees. Seaward were long leaden lanes and smoky haze and the mirage of islands in the sky.

On the river's last large island, we reached the great fur stronghold of the north, two and a half centuries old, Moose Factory — an enchanting panorama enchantingly unwinding — tepees, overturned canoes, green cultivated fields, meadows, hayricks, grazing cattle, prim cottages and rough-hewn cabins, a little old church with a leaning red tower, and in formal array, red-roofed, weatherworn post buildings.

A few curious half-breeds and their wives stood at the edge of the bank as we climbed from the landing. The men slouched, hands in pockets, gazing intently, and the women, in the abashed manner of the country, peered from the hooded depths of their plaid shawls. In the background a group of Indian women and their children lingered furtively. Dogs innumerable, enervated by the warmth of the sun, lay sprawled on the green — short-haired Indian curs, and here and there a splendid husky from the barrens of the Eskimos far northward. On the green stood an elaborately staged flagpole flanked by two old bronze field guns; adjacent, the trade shop, over its entrance the Company's emblazoned coat of arms; and deep-set from the green an old three-storied fur warehouse, alongside of it the forge of the armorer and the boatyards of the shipwrights and carpenters; and facing them all the master's white red-roofed mansion with dormer windows and a deep encircling veranda.

With the post officers — they wore informal tweeds and white collars — we dined in the messroom of the mansion, where a moccasined Indian served us from a sideboard array of old silver plate. Travel on the river, the high or low water, and such countryside topics as the approaching goose-hunting time "Hannah Bay way," Tom Pant's silver foxes, Long Mary's good-for-nothing husband, and, of course, what the free-traders were doing, were the topics of conversation. We were somewhat nonplussed that none showed more than perfunctory interest in news from the frontier or concern for the mail we had brought — toward the latter not half the avidity one of us would display toward a morning paper. It must be remembered, however, that most of these men are recruited in their teens from the Old Country. Growing up in the service from clerk apprenticeships, they become inured to the monotony of post life, its staid conventions and narrow, unchanging round of duty. One interest predominates — the Indian hunter and his fur.

Moose Factory was then the last outpost of anything like civilization, but the country Flaherty next traveled on his way to Great Whale River was not unlike the Ontario forests he had grown up in. He was still well below tree line, and the few people he met were the familiar Indians of his mining-camp days. One night, however, he had a foretaste of what was to come:

Darkness caught us while we were still sledging. Nowhere could we see a suitable place to cross the rough tidal ice which was piled high along the shore. We had to keep on. An hour passed. I was hungry and cold. Suddenly we sighted a light flickering through the darkness ahead. It was the firelight of an Indian tepee.

The bark-covered tent was filled with Indians, young and old, but they made room enough to put us up for the night. Through the evening they sat in circles round the tepee's leaping fire —

5

the old hunters, their grim, weathered faces as set as so many masks, in the first circle; the younger ones, their faces dancing in the flicker of the fire's light, on their knees behind them; and the women and children, timid and shy, hovering in the background of shadow beyond.

These Indians seldom saw white men other than traders. They watched every move I made — what I ate, how I ate, how I smoked my pipe.

"See!" exclaimed one, as I struck a match for a light. "He is too lazy to reach to the fire for a coal."

The women marvelled at my queer costume, clucked over the color of my eyes and hair.

"See!" said one. "His skin is like a child's!"

"Wait till he gets beyond the trees," said another.

"Yes," said still another, "then he will surely freeze."

"Yes," they all agreed. "He will surely freeze."

They were consumed with curiosity as to why I was undertaking such a journey. My drivers told them I was making it for no other reason than to look at the stones of a certain little island, which, if good stones, might one day be boiled over big fires and made into iron — such iron, for instance, as their guns were made of. The tepee shook with laughter. Was it possible that I believed that by boiling stones I could get iron such as their guns were made of? They had still another laughing fit when we left them in the morning.

Gradually we drew out of Indian country. On the sixth day the trees thinned out to straggling clumps. These soon gave way to solitary trees so dwarfed they looked little larger than potted plants.

At Cape Jones the Indian country came to an end. Before us lay wide panoramas of ice and snow. They were the barrens of the Eskimos. The sea coast now ran to the north and east until it was lost in the blue. In the soft light of the low sun the vast white blanket spread over land and sea like satin. Its wrinkles were blurred by snow smoke, the usual drift no matter how low the wind; for the snow of the barrens is as fine as flour and the least wind disturbs it.

6

In these drifted barrens, Robert Flaherty was to spend the better part of ten years, discovering not only islands but people, and bringing back besides his samples of iron ore a new kind of motion picture.

II. A JOURNEY FROM GREAT WHALE RIVER TO FORT CHIMO

The Hudson's Bay Company's post at Great Whale River became the starting point for several Flaherty expeditions, climaxing in February 1912, when he set out to cross the barrens of northern Ungava. His destination was Fort Chimo, at Ungava Bay on the Atlantic side, but his purpose was to search for mineral outcroppings in the great interior wilderness, an area about the size of Germany, previously known only to the Eskimos. Two previous attempts to cross the barrens, by A. P. Low and the Reverend E. J. Peck, had failed because, as Peck wrote:

> . . . we were not able to carry a large supply of provisions, but we expected to meet with reindeer and other animals which sometimes frequent these parts. In this, however, we were disappointed. For eleven days we struggled on over the frozen waste, but not a vestige of animal life could be seen. We were therefore with heavy hearts obliged to retrace our steps or perish by starvation.

Flaherty's expedition was no better provisioned, but he and his companions were lured on by tales of the vast herds of caribou which, fifty years before, had roamed the interior. With him went four Eskimos: Omarolluk and Charlie, who came for the deer they hoped to encounter; Nero, mighty hunter of the Great Whale region, who would take them as far as Lake Minto and return;

7

and Wetunik, whose well-advertised knowledge of the region beyond the lake would guide them to their destination. By mid-
March, the party had left the coast and was well on its way in
land:

March 13: They clustered about me as I hung the thermometer
on the ridge pole of the tent tonight. Of course I had to explain
it all to Nero in our amusing "Pidgin English" fashion. He in
turn explained it to his friends. But in Omarolluk couldn't understand him very well, couldn't see that if that slender thread of
mercury went down to the black mark, all water would freeze.
He was sure that the cold made water freeze, not my thermometer.

March 16: Fed the dogs on seal blubber tonight. The dogs
were tired and ravenous. Since we had no convenient way of
tying them for the night, they were free. The scene just before
feeding time was unforgettable. Omarolluk had to stand guard
with his 6-fathom whip while Wetunik cut up the blubber. The
dogs acted for all the world like wolves. They kept crawling up
on their bellies from every direction, even braving the whip, a cut
from which is certainly a painful affair. They are quick as lightning in snatching, a wolf's trait to the ground. Their fierceness
and murderous temper as the odor of the seal meat came to the
crouching circle of them is beyond telling. They foamed at the
mouth. What would happen to us without them?

March 18: Our Waldorf fare of Army rations, jam, and canned
steak will soon be exhausted, then beans forever. Nero spoke of
the flies inland, that often kill the deer. He had seen them inches
deep on the deer, the deer's face being raw and swollen by their
work. In July this happens when there are hot days and calm. He
has seen them after being killed, and says they are bloodless
through the flies' work. The Eskimos keep their dogs in their
tents during this time, imagine the smell. At one point this A.M.
we reached the summit of a portage and started descending, but
barely managed to stop short of a 75′ precipice. With our sledges
that continually strain for speed, it was no small matter to stop

8

in time. We also shortly discovered that while we were looking over for a new course, we were standing on a snow overhang which projected from the cliff about 25′. There are many snow formations like that in the rugged area here, and south along the Richmond Gulf country. The snow is everywhere wind-driven and packed to a picturesque extent, such as is not possible southward. This overhang of which I speak resembles the eave of a house on a huge scale. Many a hunter has lost his life through unconsciously walking to their edge, then suddenly breaking them off. Two men of Little Whale River Post plunged hundreds of feet to their death in that manner.

We are camped in a tiny valley, which contains a handful of stunted trees one of which is 5′ high. Camped early as the dogs are tired with their trying journey today. Do not seem to be in good condition. When we get to the deer herds they will improve again.

March 19: This entire area is barren of soil silt and trees. The rounded hills are everywhere interlaced with small lakes that are in shadow most of the day. The snow on the shadow sides of the lakes and slopes and cliffs of the hills never disappears. It truly is a desolate area. The confusing network of lakes in today's travels were too much for Wetunik, and we were consequently delayed while he climbed the hills to locate our course. At 2 P.M. we descended onto the surface of Lake Minto, though having lost the Eskimo route to it, we came onto it in strange country, so that Wetunik wasn't sure we had hit it until we travelled eastward some four or five miles and he did some further scouting on the hills. We saw two partridges, one of which Nero shot. It was given to "Beauty" tonight for supper. Would an Indian give his dog a lone partridge?

March 21: . . . Omarolluk gave further information about whales last night. He said there were many whales on the north coast, that they were black, had divided spray, white about their mouths, and were very large. These are the Ottawa Island whales of which he speaks, and other unknown islands west of Hope's Welcome. At one time the Eskimos managed to kill one and the bones of it are still there . . . This is Nero's last day with us. He turns back tomorrow for Great Whale River . . . We missed the Eskimo trail completely coming to Lake Minto, it seems, and entered it on the south side. By tonight expect to be halfway across it. We depend upon getting to deer herds, and expect to see signs of them today. At lunchtime Nero and Wetunik climbed one of the hills to look for our route, as Wetunik had become confused again. When they came down they proposed camp so that they could devote the morrow looking for the route. Made them go on however as we started late today. Wetunik located himself again. We then made for shore and camped. Camp will remain here for tomorrow. Dogs will have a rest which they need as they are very thin. Hope we get to the deer herds soon so as to get dog food. Wetunik says we are more than halfway across the lake now. Very fine day, brilliant sun which hurts my eyes very much though I wore goggles part of the time. Clear, calm. Aurora and sun dogs.

March 22: . . . Sun and snow reflection almost blinding. All but Nero off to north and south of lakes looking for deer. Nero baking bannock and fishing through ice. Hunters returned at sunset, and Wetunik saw fresh signs of about 80 deer. We push on tomorrow for east end of lake, there men will hunt for a day. Nero returns to Great Whale River tomorrow. Splendid calm and clear day. Nero drew map of lake for me in evening and we had a conference together afterwards covering route, deer herds, etc. Dog food is our greatest worry.

March 23: Said goodbye to Nero at eight o'clock and then started on our way to Fort Chimo. I felt lonesome at seeing him go. No one to speak to now. My men cannot understand a word of English and I have a vocabulary of about 25 Eskimo words. Nero will arrive at Great Whale River in about seven days' time. He's one of the most remarkable men I've ever seen. Clever, a Jap's keenness for novelty and information, the greatest hunter of his people, a daredevil on ice or in a kayak, and the model generally of all his tribe, always smiling and alert, likes to be on journeys with white men, admires them, tho' withal intensely Es-

10

kimo. Nero is an illustration of the development the Eskimos are capable of. I parted from him this A.M. with regret indeed.

Wetunik confused again and later completely lost. We have travelled some forty miles today and are now camped within two miles of last night's encampment. But are located correctly this time! The lake is a maze of long finger-bays and islands. The saucer-like hills on every side hardly vary, and it is hard to pick up landmarks. And then everything is snow and ice, with no forests to relieve the color. Distances on that account are most deceptive. Have twelve dogs in fair condition, but a very heavy load, about 800 lbs. in all.

March 24: Head wind made a disagreeable day of it. About one o'clock Wetunik became confused again and the men climbed one of the high granite hills for sight. The lake is a monster and will prove to be the largest in Labrador, not excepting Lake Messtassine, I think.

March 25: There seems to be no change in appearance of country as a whole, ever-lasting hills of granite and at wider and wider distances little patches of dwarf trees, snuggled in the valleys away from the winds. Heavy load for our dogs, one of which shows signs of giving way soon. I hope we see the deer.

March 26: Arrived at the end of the lake about 10 o'clock. The discharge is a small open rapid. We travelled on a mile further, then camped as the drift is blinding and wind very strong. Trees are increasing in size and number, and we are camped in quite a grove.

March 27: Very cold day with a typical March wind and blinding drift. Became partly snowblind, and eye is very sore indeed this evening. About 2 P.M. came across deer tracks on river ice. Omarolluk went after them and Wetunik and I went on with the team. Camped at about three o'clock and no more than had it made when Omarolluk came with the news of two deer killed. He was as happy as a child over it as he has never even seen deer

11

before, being an islander of Hope's Welcome. It means a great deal to us and nothing could have been more opportune. We all shook hands in high glee over it. The men returned at eight o'clock with the deer, cut and quartered, having given the dogs a feast while cutting them. At noon they killed two ptarmigan which they are now eating.

March 28: Laid up with snow blindness, and a painful affair it is. The men are off after the deer with dogs and sledge. It seems Omarolluk wounded one besides the ones he got. It being a very stormy day, the deer will not travel but keep in the valleys. Omarolluk killed his deer yesterday with 30.30 shells in a .303 gun. He gave me to understand the bullets were very loose. The men returned at three o'clock minus deer. At supper tonight the men tried to tell me in signs and in our very limited vocabulary that the dog I purchased from Jim Crow died today, but I thought they said they were going back to Great Whale River. For a moment was alarmed and angry, but I caught their meaning in time. Much laughter.

March 29: Our travel was most trying and were in seemingly impassable places at times. All of us done up, Wetunik with snow blindness, Omarolluk with a lame knee, and I with cramps and headache after my snow blindness. Wetunik making me a pair of Husky goggles. Cached 80 lbs. of dog food. Sledge is very heavy.

March 30: Very fine travelling and in grateful contrast to yesterday. Dogs working well after deer meat diet.

March 31: It was funny to see Omarolluk running ahead, and imitating a seal waving flippers in the air, to urge the dogs out of the ice jam we were stuck in today. Have acquired a few Eskimo words and our crazy-quilt conversations are laughable indeed.

April 1: Overcast and high southerly winds. Wetunik suffering agonies from snow blindness. Gave him some Cloridine for appearance's sake.

April 2: A late start, 9 A.M. Poor Wetunik in a bad way, cannot open his eyes and racked with headache. Have just put him in his blankets, a very sick Husky. Trouble at noon today. The men, I discovered, have been keeping their sealskin boots in my cooked-bean bag. The day is the warmest we have had. The iceing on our runners wore off quickly and part of our earthen shoeing is gone. Noted Omarolluk's method of baking bannock this evening: two handfuls of baking powder to about four pounds of flour — and we live!

April 3: Ruined our earth shoeing and had to run on the runners today. Tonight the men have made new shoeing. At feeding time one of the dogs mistook Wetunik's hand for deer meat and made a considerable mess of it. It's one damned thing after another with Wetunik. Omarolluk's knee giving him trouble.

April 4: Last evening at camp noted a Canada Jay, first bird other than the ptarmigan seen on the trip. Travel very tedious and slow owing partly to the spring day, which makes both men and dogs very sluggish. We are all on edge now, expecting and wondering when we shall come to the sea.

April 6: About 1:30 arrived at the mouth of the river. Was much surprised and delighted as were the men. The river empties into a fiord of Ungava Bay. The mouth was choked with ice and we had a very hard time of it indeed. We were from 1:30 to 6 P.M. travelling about 3 miles, and then we had to camp on sea ice and walk about a mile for a few pieces of driftwood for a fire, with the result that we did not get into our blankets until about 9:45. Very tired but happy.

April 6: One of the most trying days we have had. We camped on the sea ice last evening and broke camp this A.M. at 8 o'clock. Very soon we were into impassable and treacherous ice, where at times we had literally to chop our way. Heartbreaking work. Left the team, climbed the hillside of the mainland and saw our course was hopeless. Open water in the distance and detached floes packing shoreward. There we were, like a fly in glue. Men and dogs done up. While in the thick of the ice, a snow squall came upon us with great force and blotted out everything. Fortunately was not of long duration. Pitched camp on mainland and tomorrow will attempt to travel overland and come out on southerly side of the bay, clear of the rough ice fields.

Work tried our tempers but all right now. Omarolluk baking bannock and singing fragments of Eskimo songs, and every little while humming the tune of "Waltz Me Around Again Willie" which he has heard on some phonograph at Fort George or Great Whale River. Our very limited conversations bear altogether on Fort Chimo and our arrival.

April 7: Stuck here for the day, a miserable camp with everything wet. Men off in the hills looking for a course for our travel tomorrow. Slight snow blindness again. Wetunik went off again this P.M. to see the ice fields from the top of the range. Returned at 5:30 saying ice was all broken. Expect we shall have a hell of a time tomorrow. Omarolluk and I pouring over maps this P.M. The most miserable of all days, everything melting.

April 8: Started on our cross-country travel to avoid the rough ice fields. About 100 ptarmigan assembled on a distant knoll to see us go. Very hard and long climb to an altitude of about 600′ accomplished by noon in 100′ jobs, with the usual Husky dog conversation at each one. In the true barrens now and away from trees. One long climb was compensated by a galloping coast down the long slopes this side of the range. Encamped on the main coast of Ungava Bay with another broken ice field staring us in the face. Fort Chimo seems farther away every day.

April 9: Wetunik confused and does not know the route from here to Fort Chimo. He is certainly a useless guide and "attulie" has been his cry ever since we left Nero. It seems from what I can gather from the men that the sea coast is impossible to travel by sledge and the Ungava Bay is open water. An Eskimo route starts in from this Gulf Lake overland for Fort Chimo. As Fort Chimo is more than 75 miles away in a straight line it is most important that we find the trail. The maps are misleading *ex-*

tremely. Travelled inland no more than a mile when in a clump of trees we found a fresh Eskimo cutting. Camped, then looked for tracks underneath the soft snow, found many Eskimo tracks but none of a sledge and as yet cannot tell if these cuttings indicate a sledge or not, which is an important thing to know. The signs indicate the Eskimos have camped here about seven or eight days ago. Wetunik went off to a distant mountain to scout, but returned with no information. Our grub looking ill. Wetunik is pin head, I'm thinking. He has hunted this country and should know it. But Omarolluk makes up for him. Full of resource and brain, a "good Husky."

April 14: Westerly wind all night, heavy, still strong, less drift, partly clear. Travel fast and the excitement of nearing Fort Chimo a stimulus even to the dogs. We plied Charlie with anxious questioning all through the day trying to fix our location and nearness to the post. At about 4:30 we suddenly stood out on the last of the terraces. Fort Chimo, the great broad river, and a valley stretching to a blue haze of dazzling sun, lay before us. The white buildings of the post from our vantage looked like a strange far-off village. The descending sun shot into the innumerable windows. Bolts of light threw the surging figures of Eskimos, men and women, now aware of the arrival of a strange party, into vivid profile. The day and heat were made for our entry there, the color of sunset of the sky caught by the snow affected us strongly. The white mass of days of travel was at an end.

III. THE COLD

The journey from Great Whale River to Fort Chimo was an early one, spurred by the hope of mineralogical discoveries and the zest for exploration. Both motives continued to dominate Flaherty's work for Sir William Mackenzie during the next eight years, but to them another slowly added itself — an absorbed contemplation of the land and the people for their own sake. The diaries, an endless soliloquy, muse forever on the wonderful fact of Eskimo survival and joy of life in a country whose harshness was a continual test of endurance and of the will to live itself.

In several books, Vilhjalmur Stefansson has portrayed the "friendly" Arctic as a land of abundance, where staying alive was a fairly simple matter. Flaherty never found it so. Here, as nowhere he had been or was to go, nature, the natural condition of things, was an unwinking and implacable enemy. The malice of the white North might with good excuse have made any man, or race of men, turn his face to the wall and die. Yet the Eskimos did not. How? Why? Flaherty asked himself.

The determining fact of the North was the cold.

The predominant hardship of this travel [Flaherty noted in 1914] is the tedious and chilly waiting while our Eskimos are building the igloos. They take the better part of an hour while we have nothing to do but stamp cold feet and rub noses and look on. Simonie and our new man travel without sleeping bags, simply lie down to sleep on a winter deer-skin robe, though I fancy their night's sleep is broken with innumerable short naps. Simonie awakened Sam at 4 A.M. saying that the early morning frost would cover the salt rime to some extent, which of course would make the sledge travel easier. Of course this was an excuse as Simonie and the new man weren't comfortable minus sleeping bags and felt the cold night. Our igloo was built too small and proved very uncomfortable. Imagine it was very cold, but thank God I stopped carrying thermometers, which are altogether too stimulating to one's imagination.

Igloos might be cold, but they were equatorial compared to the murderous cold of the outdoors. Eight years later, while making his first film, Flaherty wrote:

By the time we reached the crest the wind was running wild. Nanook went off to locate igloo snow. I crouched behind the bulwark of the sledge and watched the towers and spirals and jets

16

of drift bound from ledge to ledge, from slope to slope down to the ice foot, a white hair-line nine hundred feet below. Never did Nanook's spiral of snow blocks build up so slowly. Before the first tier was up I was crouched behind it and Nanook with his snow knife cut off a hunk of snow and tried to rub the white of my frozen cheeks and nose. By the time the last block was set, black night was down. Nanook and the crew fed the dogs, coiled the harnesses, and sealed up the igloos' door. I had camp all made. The moss wick of the seal oil lamp was sending off heart-warming little tongues of flame; hunks of snow in the pot above it were melting and warming up for scalding draughts of tea. Frozen seal meat and my beans were thawing; the willow mats were down, and the sleeping bags lay unrolled on the igloo's floor of snow. When Nanook had thawed out his frozen white nose and whiter cheeks and rubbed them red again, said he, his arms sweeping round the sparkling white dome that sheltered us: "Oh surely no igloo of the kablunak is so wonderful!" I agreed.

The cold was like a new and unknown element which transformed the familiar ones. Air was changed into something almost tangible which burned the lungs like a fiery draught, and water, which the rest of the world freezes to chill its food, had here to be thawed over flame to make it drinkable. Except for a few weeks of summer or on the open sea, it was never to be seen in liquid form. It was no longer water but ice, a solid, and it was, after the cold itself, the most important fact of life for the Eskimos.

IV. THE ICE

Their lives were governed by it. In winter, the frozen sea was their highroad—sledging on its surface being much smoother than on land, except when the winds and tides had created areas of jam ice: "huge blocks, often 40 feet high, deserted by the ebb tide in topsy-turvy postures, clumps of profiles and ice-battlemented designs whose fantasy increases as you gaze and peer at

17

them." In summer the quickest way to travel was by boat along the shoreline, and ice, no longer a means of travel, became a menace. Suppose, for example, you were paddling a canoe in the sea with companions and you met an iceberg:

We passed a group of bergs. They were wandering willy-nilly on the tide. One loomed high above the rest. The strata of gulls which encircled its hoary head looked like specks. The sun was warm. Emerald streams of water cascaded over the berg's flanks. Then a miracle happened. With a yawn the giant began to turn over. Slowly its weather-soiled slopes sank into the sea. The crew yelled with dismay. We swung the canoe and fled, for the rings of swells which began to race out from it were gigantic, big enough, we feared, to swamp us, though we were a mile or more away. Over the top of the little rocky island which lay some half-way between us and the turning monster the ring of swells, when they struck, completely overwhelmed it, and with a tremendous roar swept a block of stranded ice from its crest into the sea.

"Quick!" cried Nawri. "Swing!" as the first of the swells came galloping toward us. We faced it just in time. As it struck, the canoe leaped so high that from bow to amidships the bottom was in the air and the stern for an instant under water. For miles around white water broke over rocks of islands, and furiously tossed and tumbled the ice-pans which had been peacefully drifting on the smooth glass of the sea. Walrus barked; seals shot up their astonished heads.

When we looked toward the berg again the miracle was complete — the new face that rose to displace the old was more blue than sapphire, more green than emerald, and adrip with water that glinted in the sun like drops of molten gold.

We paddled on into the north. Hours later, as we were rounding a point of land, we saw the last of it far out at sea, sailing proudly like a swan. It still looked gigantic, for its reflection doubled it. The gem-like facets of its new-born flanks ran the gamut of every shade of blue and green and shot back still the fire of the dying sun.

Or suppose that, like Nanook, you were out hunting on the summer ice when it parted and the wind drove the ice pack you were on out into the vastness of Hudson Bay:

Where it happened is not a half day's sledging from his igloo. We were out on the rough ice after bear. We had made a kill and were on our way in to land when we came upon a lane of open water which stood between us and the ice foot of the Cape. Far off in the distance the lane narrowed. We dropped our kill and made off as fast as we could travel, but nowhere was the lane narrow enough to leap. Just in time we spied an ice-pan. It was about the length of a sledge. With the ice-pan for a boat, our harpoons for paddles, we paddled across.

Then each of the crew told of some misadventure he had had at some time or other on the ice. "Harry Lauder," with his father and mother, the mother carrying a babe in arms, were adrift all through one moon off the Gulf Hazard coast. When the west winds packed the icefield in to the mainland, where they landed was Cape Dufferin, two hundred and fifty miles north of Gulf Hazard. The winter was almost done before they saw home again.

V. THE DOGS

The primitive Eskimo is constantly on the move. In the summer he may settle down for a few weeks beside a salmon-stocked stream, venturing occasionally into the interior after deer, while his family overhaul their communal possessions. But all the rest of the year he must move on from day to day in an unending search for game. Woe to the family which, in the dead of winter, loses its sledge, by which alone can be transported the weapons, deer-, bear- and sealskins, and the few pots and lamps which are their all in all. And woe indeed to the family whose dogs die or are killed. For without a sledge, and dogs to pull it, the Eskimo cannot cover with enough speed the scores and even hundreds of

19

miles which may lie between the breathing-holes of the seal in the sea ice, or the sparse and hidden dens of the bear.

All through the ten years of the diaries, at dawn and sundown and through days of travel, the dogs thread in and out of the story:

. . . The next day we fished around the ice edge of the open rapid, but we neither saw nor caught a fish. We had constant reminders of the hunger of the dogs — the poor brutes were starving. Every little while they broke into a fight, and they fought to kill. With whips and snowshoes and clubs we kept them from annihilating one poor brute that for two days past had been slowly breaking and could no longer keep his trace taut. We had to feed him separately, for though he was one of the biggest of all the dogs he was too weak any longer to defend himself. Omarolluk shook his head as he swept his hand across the dog's ribs.

"No use," he said, "tomorrow we must cut him out of the team and let him follow us. If we don't, by nightfall he may be gone."

"Wouldn't it be better to kill him," I suggested, "and feed him to the other dogs?"

Omarolluk said his meat was too lean to give any comfort to the bellies of the other dogs; such starved meat would only make them sick.

"Never mind," he went on hopefully. "Maybe soon we will come to other rapids down the river, and the next time maybe we will get fish."

"Yes, and maybe not!" said Wetunik.

. . . We had not gone far when the leader of the team, a beautiful little wolf-gray bitch, lay down and refused to rise. She whined and licked her paws when Omarolluk and I went up to her. We had to unharness her, put her on top of the sledge, and lash her to the load. She and I had been good friends, and so I saved little tidbits of food and gave them to her. This pampering aroused the ire of Omarolluk. If she was spoiled, he said, she would be little use to him as leader of the team. There was no other dog half so good to take her place as leader if we had to sledge over broken ground, where one scrape against a boulder would rip off our good earthen shoeing. What would we do when we struck rough ice? "Truly," he declared, "without a good leader we will lose days, and this is not the best land to lose them in. Is it not so?"

That night in camp Omarolluk made deerskin moccasins for the leader's feet, for they had been badly cut by ice. The next morning she gamely tackled her task again with a moccasin tied on each foot; but in a little while she played out again. Again we took her aboard the sledge. She was singularly friendly for an Eskimo dog. I had often wondered why, until Wetunik said that as a puppy she had never run with the pack, but instead had grown up in the factor's house at Great Whale. Omarolluk said he had never driven a better leader; it was wonderful how well she worked in rough ice where the twists and turns were often so abrupt that at the end of her 100-foot-long trace she could not be seen. Even so she could always hear the slightest utterance of Omarolluk, his "ouk" and "arah," and twist and turn exactly as he wanted her.

. . . The rough-and-tumble played out the dogs. When Omarolluk and Wetunik returned from a fruitless day's search for deer, hardly one of the dogs had energy enough left to break out from its blanket of drifted snow. Their night's rest did them little good, for when we started on the journey again we could hardly urge them on. A bitch of our team gave birth to a pup last night, and one at noon today as she ran, the latter being promptly torn to pieces and eaten by the following dogs in harness. These premature births are caused by intense cold, say the Eskimos. I think hard work on the sledge has something to do with it.

Constantly our eyes roved for signs of game, scanning the nooks and crannies of the drift-swept hills and the grooves of the valleys that wound among them down to the river's shore, and among the straggling clumps of spectral trees; but on all that hopelessness of white and gray all that lived and breathed and moved were our own black dots, bending slowly over the loops and curves of the endless stream.

21

I was beginning to wonder whether the dogs, which had been left in the care of Wetunik, would go hungry, when from the outside came the crunch, crunch of footsteps. It was Nero and his helper, their arms piled high with spruce. They soon had a fire blazing before the igloo, and over it they hung the huge kettle with its seal-blubber and corn-meal, mixed with snow. Our 25 dogs formed a ring round the leaping flames, lying down with paws outstretched. In the flickering firelight their mad eyes gleamed like molten coals. White spume covered their hungry jaws. They were too tense to give tongue.

When the cooking was done and it was time to dump the scalding mess out upon the snow, three men had to ply their long whips constantly to keep the maniacal circle back. But the dogs, just out of reach of the cracking whips, kept circling, belly-down, like the wolves they were. They knew well enough that the lashes would cut clean through their hide, split an ear, or put out an eye. But one or another poor devil took the cut before he was backed out of range. They were too intent to fight save when one of them was caught by the lash. The pain of it would send him bounding straight in the air, or maddened beyond all control he would bury his fangs in the unfortunate nearest him.

When at last the big round splatter of dog-food lay cold upon the snow, the drivers jumped out of harm's way and the dogs like lightning leaped in. The meal was over in thirty seconds. After the feast there was one last fight, but not a serious one — for the dogs were never so dangerous after being fed — before they bedded themselves in the snow for their long night's sleep.

When I came out of doors for a last look around before turning in, the ground drift had already covered them. Only the black tips of their noses stuck up through the snow.

. . . The dogs had been failing rapidly. One of them the night before had broken into a grub-box and fished out of it a five-pound sealed tin of lard. In ripping it open he had got a piece of the tin jammed in his teeth. Nero and Omarolluk had had to pin him to the snow and wrench it out of his bleeding jaws. Some of the other dogs had tried to get at the sealskin thongs which bound

22

the cross-pieces on one of the sledges. "We must get red meat soon," said Nero.

. . . The drivers were up and out before daybreak. First there were the sledges to get ready — two 14-foot-long brutes with black spruce runners 2 inches thick. It was all I could do to break one of the sledges from its tracks and pull it a few feet along the snow. This abnormal weight was not all timber; the shoeing accounted for some of it. The shoeing was not steel. Steel would be out of the question in this latitude, where, due to the extreme cold, there is little moisture in the snow; over this extremely dry snow steel runners would track no better than over sand. Actually the shoeing was fashioned of frozen brown-black peat dug up from the muskegs. This peat, after being cleared of small sticks and stones, was mixed with water into a paste and then moulded by hand onto each sledge runner, freezing, of course, as soon as it was laid. This moulded shoeing, half round in shape, is from 2 to 2½ inches thick; in cross-section it looks like a piece of steel rail.

But it is not the surface of this elaborate construction that tracks over the frozen sea and the snow-packed wastes. Even this peat-shoeing, though it is smoothed and polished until it resembles a piece of polished mahogany, would stick too much. Like cures like. The actual shoeing must be ice.

And that was what the drivers were doing now. The sledges lay belly-up in the snow before them. With their hands the drivers smoothed the shiny brown half-round shoeing, and then from a pail of snow water which they had melted in the igloo they took huge mouthfuls and began squirting a fine spray through their teeth upon the runner surfaces, smoothing with one hand the spray which almost instantly congealed to ice. Up and down the 14 foot lengths of the runners they kept on squirting these fine jets of spray. In a few moments the sledge runners were shining white with ice.

While two helpers packed the sledges and lashed the waist-high loads, one by one the black tips of the dogs' noses began to stir, and they broke out of their berths under the snow, stood up, stretched, shook off the snow and stood patiently while the drivers put on their sealskin harnesses. The dogs seemed more dead than alive, yawning and shivering until the long trace of each of them was fastened to the master line.

Then the excitement began. While we gave a last pull here and there to the seal thong lashings of the bulging loads, up shot the thick bushy tails until they stood straight as cockades. The dogs lunged wildly at the ends of their long traces, the whole wide fan of them. We could hardly hear each other speak, such a din they made as they leaped and strained and tugged to be off.

"Tiamak! Are you ready?" called Nero. The drivers took a last look at the sealskin thongs which lashed the sledge-loads. The loads were as carefully tied and cinched as a cowboy's saddle.

"Tiamak!" they yelled in answer.

Nero unlimbered his six-fathom whip. The roars and howls of the dogs were deafening. Nero's whip resounded like a rifle shot. All shoulders shoved at the sledge-loads to break out the heavy sledges. With a rush we started. The waist-high loads, to one of which I clung, began to roll as the sledges sped forward like ships on a choppy sea.

It was all a bluff, however, this first break of the dogs to get away. Could they keep up such a pace, the wide interior which we faced would be crossed in a dozen days. Within a few hundred yards, the heavy loads told, and the dogs settled down into the business of dragging behind them the monstrous things that would all but burst their hearts when they tried to pull them up a steep slope, and when they were going down the other side would, if they were not careful, over-run them and drag them helpless behind, with muzzles and legs together ploughing deep through the snow. They had to settle too to the dreary business of dragging, over the level ground, the two-legged creatures, whose long whips, like red-hot bullets, would make them leap straight into the air with pain.

Now they were in their stride, the steady pit-pat of the trot, just fast enough to make the two-legged ones break their clumsy gait and trot as well. They must keep on trotting, never to stop, unless the two-legged ones ran before them with a whip and forced them to halt while traces were untangled, sledge runners re-iced, or particles of ice removed from between the toes of some dog's bleeding feet. Yes, keep on trotting, and bite deep the dog, no matter if he was played out, that lagged. For with the night would come their food. Food! That indeed was what they had been howling and crying and lunging for at the start in the morning.

VI. "THE ESKIMOS ARE SOLELY HUNTERS AND FISHERS"

DEER: 1912 . . . Three deer reported about one and one-half miles away on the south shore. I sorted out ammunition and we went after them over small uplands and broad valleys and around tundra-bordered pools and ponds. At noon sighted them to the northeast about a mile away. Palliack, Nami, Long Hair, and Partridge worked into them, the remainder spreading out south of the valley, in case they took alarm. Not long before the shooting commenced. They literally poured lead into them with repeating rifles. Two cows and a bull. Noted that their winter coats were still on and horns in velvet. Palliack easily plucked the winter coat off and obtained a splendid summer deerskin for himself. In short order the men had them cut up and packed in their own skins, strips of the hide being cut with which to tie the whole and pack them. Nucky was busy breaking open the leg joints and knuckles and eating the marrow with gusto.

Returned about three o'clock to find our harbor a raging river of rapids in islands of boulders. The women were scattered about the granite ledge in various degrees of dress amid a rubble of dishes and cooking gear. Sundry articles of their personal adornment were plastered to boulders, drying. We are a happy family surely! The sun is hot, the rocks reflect it and we are bathing in it, awaiting in lazy apathy the flood tide.

The first flies today in considerable number, but not biting. Noted that we saw none till we came up with the deer.

1912 . . . Hours passed. Desperately I tried to keep awake, straining my ears for the tell-tale crunch of snow. Now and then a dog would whine. The drifter droned. Midnight came. I had to crawl deep into my eiderdown sleeping bag or freeze. It was inevitable — I fell asleep.

I was dreaming. There were deer — a thousand deer — but it was summer — they were swimming across the river. We didn't kill them — we were tired of deer meat; we wanted fish, fish that we could catch through the ice. But there was no ice. Where was the ice? Where were the dogs to take us to the ice? There were no dogs — the dogs were dead.

Something fell over me; something was shaking my shoulder. My eyes opened. It was Wetunik.

Every dog was howling as he had never howled since the seal meat days on Hudson Bay. I sat up. I was wide awake now.

"Listen!" said Wetunik.

The crunch, crunch of footsteps resounded on the snow. A moment later Omarolluk's head was framed in the door. My eyes blinked. Was he mad? He was smiling! He held up one hand before his face.

"Pingashoot!" he cried, showing us three fingers. "Pingashoot!"

"You killed three?" I exclaimed incredulously.

"Ae," he answered. "There was much drift. I got very close. There were five deer. I killed three!"

We were too hungry for the good red meat to wait upon the day.

"Don't cook for us," said Omarolluk. "Wetunik and I will make out all right."

Before them on the floor lay a haunch of deer meat. With stones they were whetting the foot-long steel knives I had got for them at Great Whale. Both Primus lamps were going full blast. On one, snow was thawing in the kettle for tea-water. On the other was frying the most precious piece of venison it has ever been my lot to eat.

"Are you fellows sure you don't want some of the deer meat cooked?" I asked.

"No, no," they protested together. "We're all right. Our way is the best for the Innuit."

They had cut the haunch, and now each had a piece of raw meat before him larger than his head. Their knives were razor-sharp, but they did not employ them, as we use a table knife, to

26

cut the meat into small pieces. They only used them to lop off the dangling edges of the huge chunks of meat which they crammed into their mouths. Each cut almost shaved their lips — indeed, one slip of the knife might well have cut off the end of a nose.

"We have no room in our mouths for words!" exclaimed the ravished Wetunik, between pieces.

"Ae," sighed blissful Omarolluk. He added, though it took much effort, that beans might be best for the kablunak, but the good tooktoo was best for him.

"Ae," squealed Wetunik.

My own fried steak of venison was soon dispatched, and not long afterwards I fell asleep.

Some time later I woke up. A light was still burning. I looked for Omarolluk and Wetunik. Though their slant eyes were almost closed, their long knives were still cutting off the good red tooktoo close to their mouths.

When I awoke in the morning they were as still as two logs. I called to them, but neither heard. I knew then that they wouldn't be up for hours to come.

The igloo was bitterly cold, but such was the heat they had won from their raw meat gorge that their prostrate forms were covered with hoar frost and little clouds of steam rose up from them into the frigid air.

1912 . . . For four days we continued eastward over the ice of Kasagaleek. The only break in the monotony of low, barren granite shores was the skeleton of a tepee frame — a gaunt silhouette against the sky — an old camp of Indians who used to come here in the few short weeks of summer from their own hunting grounds within the limit of trees, far southward. At another place Nero pointed out the spot where, when he was a boy, his father had made a deer kill — so many, said he, that it had taken three days to cut them up. Here as everywhere through the great interior, Nero continued, the Eskimos used to come in from the coast in the early spring, on the watch for deer migrations as they worked north from the Indian's land of trees. Sometimes there were so many that if one put his ear to the ground he could hear them. "Him sound like thunder, very; but now," lamented Nero, "deer, him gone. Husky — him starve."

He spoke of three families who, several winters before, had struck out from the Koksoak across the interior in search of deer. "Nobody saw 'um no more."

WALRUS: 1911 . . . Our whale-boat was making its way through the ice-floes off shore. Flocks of eiders from rock ledges of the shore rose in alarm as we approached, and in whirring flights circled us. The screams of gulls were constantly in the air. A herd of walrus, holding to the edge of a drifting ice pan with their gleaming tusks, let go and with a resounding splash dived from view.

"The walrus is bad when he is angry," Wetalltok said. "That same summer one Eskimo went out from shore with his kayak to hunt ducks. Though early in the morning there had been a walrus kill, there were no signs of walrus then. He did not come back. All that the people could find were pieces of kayak. The water was red, red, red.

"And you have heard of that kablunak (a member of the Northwest Mounted Police at Cape Fullerton). Their whaleboat was strong and big, but the walrus they had wounded with their gun but did not kill swam under the boat and up over the side. With his tusks he turned it over. Two of the kablunak swam in to shore, which was near, but the other one was frightened. He swam out. The two kablunak who got on shore saw the walrus charge the kablunak who was swimming. The walrus kept on charging him, even after he was dead. Then he went for the boat and smashed it to pieces with his tusks. And then he charged the pieces which floated in the sea."

BEAR: 1912 . . . Breakfast at six. Fog clear at 6:30. Have had the best sailing weather of the trip, but very cold and uncomfortable. About 11 A.M. while sailing along the lee side of a large floe, Nami suddenly shouted, "Nanook! Nanook!" Just some polar bear a hundred yards ahead. I saw him swimming for the floe; he landed in short order, galloped across it and took to the water again, we sailing for him with a beam wind and large sea

28

running. Overhauled him shortly and headed for the shore. Crew now took in the sail, and we followed the more slowly swimming fellow with paddles, keeping a respectful fifty feet or so behind him. I got out both cameras and went up near the bow. Asked the men to close in a little more, which they reluctantly did, until our quarry came around with a snort, whereupon we fell back to the old margin. Much surprised he did not swim faster, didn't seem to have nearly the speed that a moose has. Men waited with rifles ready, and as he landed I took my pictures while they fired. Ambrose fired first with his ".22" in order to bay him on the rocks, but Nami and Nucky followed too quickly and spoiled my chance for a most interesting picture. They at once started in skinning and cutting up the carcass, Nucky and I getting dinner ready. The bear is a fair size and in good condition. Taking pelt and skull and part of the meat.

Eight P.M. Southeast wind, cloudy and cold. Ice is packing in shore rapidly. Saw many seal and one white whale, which went by us at 50 feet. The men regretted that their guns were not in readiness, but for my part was glad as we are surfeited with seal, whale, and bear meat, and salmon trout. Have made a splendid run. All through the balance of our day's travel every peculiarly shaped outline on the ice floes was a bear.

1920 . . . He went on to describe how in early December the she-bear dens in huge drift banks of snow. There is nothing to mark the den save a tiny vent or air-hole which is melted open by the animal's body heat. "Three winters ago on the Cape," said Nanook, "there were many, many bear. One night the snarling and yelping of the dogs in the igloo tunnel woke me. In the igloo, head and shoulders through the door, was a bear. He had come in through the snow tunnel. Behind him the dogs were biting and snapping at his legs and haunches; he could not back out and he could not come through. My harpoon and spears were outside. I must cut a hole through the igloo walls; but the walls — it was an old igloo — were almost ice. The bear was growling, showing his teeth — his lips were all foam. If the dogs would let him he would smash down the door. I cut through the igloo wall and got my spear. My family were frightened."

29

Then "Harry Lauder" said: "Annunglung and his mother (Annunglung's father was dead) killed a bear last winter on the Kogaluk. Annunglung is only a boy. He and his mother were going from the igloo to the river's mouth to fish. They met a bear. They wanted that bear, for they were hungry. But all they had was a bow and arrows. The dogs brought the bear to a stand. Annunglung shot all his arrows, but he did not kill the bear. They had nothing left. They wanted the bear, for they were very, very hungry. One arrow was sticking in the bear; the others were near him on the ground. Annunglung, to fool the bear, jumped toward his head, and his mother ran in. With one hand she grabbed the arrows on the ground. With the other she grabbed the arrow sticking in the bear. They killed the bear."

SEAL: 1915 . . . Awoke at 9:30. Light head winds. Started about 11 o'clock. The two boats drifted along with fitful rowing at times by the women. The men in their kayaks scooted along the mirror surface of the water, and in amongst the ice floes after seal and ducks. They had a great seal hunt which took an hour or so of chasing and maneuvering for the spear-throwing at the seal. It was much like the coon hunting of the Indian. When the seal rose to the surface, all of them in chorus kept up a great noise, which in the distance sounded like a ball game at home. This row kept the seal in curiosity until an Eskimo in his speedy kayak got his chance for a throw. However, there were many dives and throws and misses before Annotook hit his mark. We all straightaway proceeded to an ice cake, where the seal was carved. The dogs formed the outer circle of interested spectators. Every part of the seal was used for dogs and men. Partridge, as chief, offered me the liver and a bit of seal pup that had been killed earlier in the day. I accepted diplomatically, and told my tummie not to butt in. They poured the blood into a sealskin bag, stretched out the skin to dry, and made fires on the ice cake and boiled some of the meat. We have anchored, 11 P.M., to a floe for the night, or rather through the twilight.

1912 . . . These summer days are not travelling days. Again there were many seals, waterfowl, and schools of salmon trout.

The sea was burnished steel and silver, which caught the heavy cloud shadows and mirrored the glinting green and white ice floes. We couldn't paddle continuously, the warm sun and languid air, with innumerable seals large and small popping their heads up at close range, proved too distracting. After several volleys of spattered lead had missed several seal, as a joke I asked Jimmy if he was really "Kokpoonganetsuk" (hungry for seal). When he answered with that smile of his, I said, "Very well, your master will kill one for you. Now, you see that small one over there — call him!" Borrowed Ambrose's cheap little "trade .22" which we've all (but Ambrose) taken turns at ridiculing. Waited, expecting to miss so badly that the absurdity of it would convulse them. The seal came up at 75 yards. I fired. An exclamation from the crew made me realize I had become sublimely wonderful to them. Not only did I hit that seal, but killed him instantly. The only spirited paddling of the day occurred just then to reach him before he sank. Whether they were more pleased at the feast to come or amazed at the freak affair would be hard to say. Took full advantage of this chance to tease them unmercifully. We landed on a large ice floe later on for water, and took pot shots at several seal (nary a pot).

VII. "THE GOVERNMENT IS MAINLY A FAMILY ONE"

1914 . . . Whilst in the midst of dinner Simonie and his wife returned from his walrus hunt and exerted themselves to show us their hospitality and welcome. Simonie is one of the finest type of Baffinland Eskimo, a mighty hunter, which here means affluence and plenty. The criterion to his prowess is the fact that he heads two domestic establishments, in which he alternates his residence day by day. He is young and exceedingly active, a handsome type, very popular with his people. He shows singular enterprise, perhaps audacity, in taking his 19-year-old wife with him walrus hunting, which of all things is a mighty cold and dangerous job. They hover about the edge of the set icefields 9 miles or so distant from land, awaiting an opportunity to creep up to close quarters with a two-ton walrus asleep along the edge of the ice fields. The greater danger is that of the icefields breaking into sheets and moving out with the enormous tides so peculiar to this coastline, with its strong, steady, circular currents that sweep through Hudson Strait to the Atlantic, which would carry them oceanward in a short time indeed. Simonie harpooned a walrus today as he lay sleeping along the ice edge with only his head above water, secured to the ice by his tusk. In some instances one can approach without the least fear of his awakening. The great idea in walrus hunting is to harpoon him before shooting, as otherwise in most cases he sinks before a line and float can be attached. Simonie was successful in securing him, but found it impossible to haul him up onto the ice, though there were other hunters with him. He severed his head and had to be content with that as the result of his hard day's work.

VIII. "GENERAL GOOD FELLOWSHIP MARKS THEIR RELATIONS"

1912 . . . Have struck up companionship with Palliack's 3-year-old son, and as he hasn't arrived at the fluent stage of his own language yet, we hit it off very well. Showed him my safety razor, and after seeing me shave he intimated that he wanted to be shaved, which I proceeded to do amid great laughter from the circle of onlookers. His mother showed signs of anxiousness during the operation. He knows all about my biscuits, syrups, and canned fruits. Took him into cabin and gave him a half can of raspberries and biscuit, which put him way off his seal meat and milk diet (for according to Eskimo custom he was still at his mother's breast). Happily he came around again in a short time and greeted me with his quaint "O Kahurie" when I came up to the tent this morning.

1912 . . . Nero was famous throughout the country as the one Eskimo who could speak a few words of the white man's tongue. "Me no speak much, only few," was the way he put it. His face was frank and friendly and his slant eyes sparkled. He looked after me as though I were a child. To bare my hands in the bitter wind long enough to strike a match was more than I could any longer do, for within a few seconds my fingers would become so numb that the lighted match would drop. Nero performed this service for me; he also valeted my furs (I was dressed in deerskin like the Eskimos); at turning-in time at night he pulled off my sealskin boots with his teeth, and at rising time in the morning he softened the frozen soles of them so that I could pull them on.

1912 . . . First giving me a short club with which to threaten any dogs I might have to pass, Nero told me to follow him. On hands and knees we crawled some 20 feet through a long, low tunnel, and then, squeezing through a door, came into a large igloo, the dome of which was several feet higher than our heads. Two thirds of its round floor was taken up by a knee-high bench of hard, wind-packed snow on top of which were spread mats of creeping willows and robes of deerskin. At one end of this snow-bench sat the housewife, her naked babe nestled warmly in the depths of her kooletah along her naked back, for the voluminous hood of the kooletah, which in the cold out-of-doors is pulled up over the head, was now turned down. The chin of the baby rested on its mother's bare shoulder. It looked up at me unafraid, with wondering eyes. The mother was trimming her lamp — a foot-long narrow basin made of soapstone and filled with seal oil. One side of the lamp was quarter-round and the other straight; at this straight edge burned several feeble flames, the wicks of which were moss. The mother turned from the trimming of one of the moss wicks which with the others lit the sparkling white cavern with a feeble yellow light, and, smiling, welcomed us. Her babe poked out its tiny naked arm for my hand to grasp, and, still unafraid, smiled.

A nest of yelping puppies snuggled in a furlined niche of the igloo's snow wall. All the puppies in winter were kept within the igloo, Nero told me, for if they once got outside some starving big dog would be sure to eat them.

Nero spread out my eiderdown sleeping bag upon the snow platform in a space the housewife pointed out to him. He then helped me off with my deerskin kooletah, which he handed to the housewife. With a short club she beat from it the powdered snow which after my long day's travel through the snow-smoke was lodged like fine dust in the fur. It is very necessary to get this powdered snow out of one's furs as soon as an igloo is entered, for if the temperature of the igloo rises a little the snow powder will soon melt, only to freeze later when it is exposed to the cold again, the fur becoming stiff and unwieldy as so much tin. The housewife then pulled off my knee-long sealskin boots and put them on the rack over her lamp. Their stiff soles she would chew soft when I awoke in the morning.

The housewife was astonished at the efficiency of my blow-lamps with their bright blue flames. How much better they were, she exclaimed, than her own feeble lamp! It took hours for her to melt water from the snow, she said, so stupid was her lamp.

In the meantime the housewife got Nero's meal ready, simply cutting off a huge portion of raw meat from the frozen seal carcass that lay before her on the snow floor. Under all conditions an Eskimo prefers seal meat to any food the white man can offer. As Nero said, "Seal, him best food and make more warm too." Then, to prove it: "It's me that lights your pipe for you in the cold wind, is it not? Your hand no good for cold."

1911 . . . When Christmas came we kept open house for Wetalltok and his throng, and all the islanders who were camped nearby. Salty Bill improvised a tree. Spruce boughs, which he had brought up from Moose for the purpose of making spruce beer, he lashed to a pole. The candles were foot-long miner's dips, and the decorations were brightly labelled fruit cans from the cook's scrap pile. The presents were black plug tobacco and matches for the men, and needles and combs and trade candy for the women and their flocks. While Bill acted Santa Claus, Wetalltok's gramophone belched forth its rasping sounds. The lilt of "Tipperary" and of Harry Lauder's songs was contagious, but the "Preacher and the Bear," with its monologue and the realistic growling from a supposed bear, was a knockout.

"Nanook! Nanook!" ("the bear! the bear!") they exclaimed, rocking with laughter, but the kiddies, half-frightened, clung to their mothers and rolled their almond eyes.

When the ceremonies around the tree were over, Bill herded

the teddy-bear youngsters around the stove and popped corn, the most surprising thing by way of food they had ever seen. "Cakeot nucky" (the gun food) they called it, as, enraptured, they watched the kernels popping in the air.

1912 . . . A blizzard now and very cold. One needs winter clothing the year through. Good old Partridge noted me shiver while writing this, and straightaway fetched me one of his koole-tahs, all washed and clean, and let me understand it was a present. These people are considerate of my comfort. How such kindness is valued up here, away from everything, can be imagined.

Several seal alarms during the day, but nothing killed. To hear the excited Huskies gesticulating and hurrying to and fro for their guns, the good wife not the least active, with youngsters bobbing in her hood like tourists on a camel — the rapid launching and the scooting of those shark-nosed kayaks to the rings of the water of the seal's last dive — spears poised and ready — is not easily forgotten.

1912 . . . At noon decided to go the balance of the journey by canoe. I felt sorry to say goodbye to my old friends. Of the Eskimos who came away with me, Nami is the silent steady chap with the strength of a bull, Ambrose, the comedian, though all his subtle brilliant work is in un-understandable Eskimo. Nucky is bow and captain — the early riser and the sooth-sayer. Heaven knows we need an early riser and therefore he is in many ways our prima donna. Augchick, Partridge's son, is the youngster of the outfit. To see his kind old mother packing his duffle — with bits of advice here and there — his father looking on silently, though reinforcing his mother's words, is for all the world the same as we have it. His young wife of about 17 and their son went aboard with the first canoe, so that she didn't figure in the final farewells; I guess she felt it, though. I shall never get over finding out the goodness of these people. . . .

IX. *NANOOK OF THE NORTH*

For Flaherty, to find out something was to feel the urge to proclaim it to all the world. In an earlier time, proclamation might have taken the form of those traveler's tales and chronicles of exploration which men like Flaherty have poured out through the ages. But a new instrument of storytelling was at hand. When Flaherty excitedly declaimed his enthusiasm for Eskimo life to his employer, the ever-receptive Sir William agreed that he should take a movie camera along with him on his next expedition. Thus the Baffinland and Belcher Islands expeditions were filmed in fragmentary fashion, and the negative, miraculously surviving a thousand hazards, arrived safely in Toronto. Egged on and aided by his wife, Flaherty spent a winter editing the reels into a semblance of narrative. One afternoon, after all the work was done, he was packing the cut negative to send it to New York. A cigarette fell off a table-top into some scrap film on the floor and, in minutes, the entire negative exploded into flame. The injudicious smoker, who tried to beat out the fire with his hands, barely escaped with his life and was hospitalized for weeks.

> We still had a positive print of the film [he said] and we took it to New York in the hope of getting it duplicated. We were unsuccessful; it wasn't possible, in those days, to make a duplicate negative from a positive. But in the course of getting around we showed the print a good deal — at the American Geographic Society, at the Explorers' Club in New York, and to friends at our home in New Canaan, Connecticut. People were polite, but I could see that what interest they took in the film was the friendly one of wanting to see where *I* had been and what *I* had done. That wasn't what I wanted at all. I wanted to show the Innuit. And I wanted to show them, not from the civilized point of view, but as they saw themselves, as "we the people." I realized then that I must go to work in an entirely different way.*

The print of this film, the first study for *Nanook of the North,*

* "I made the same mistake nearly everybody has made. But something quite different is needed. I am too old for it, isn't it a pity?"—Eleonora Duse, on making her first film.

has disappeared. If any reader knows where it is hiding, he will make a contribution to film history by bringing it to light. It must have been very like the films which globe-trotters have been making monotonously from 1900 till today, and which rarely appear on the screen except in that form of short travelogue with which everyone is familiar and which no one wants to see. In these films the wonderfully flexible machine of the motion picture is used as though it were simply a box camera for taking snapshots. They emphasize the *strangeness* of foreign lands and peoples, and what they like to dwell on is the sensational or *outré,* when they are lucky enough to happen on it. Flaherty's drive was in the opposite direction. He wanted to reveal how like us the Eskimos were, not how unlike. His first film showed him his mistake; he had plumped for the picturesque, when what he needed were the dramatic, aspects of Eskimo life. To correct this became an obsession. Minerals, exploration, and the self-important doings of the civilized world, meant nothing. He must go back to the North.

But how? The First World War was then drawing near its end, but all energies, and all finance, were still being poured into its maw. There was no economic reason for going back. Then Flaherty met Captain Thierry Mallet of the fur-trading firm of Revillon Frères. Revillon had just decided to give the Hudson's Bay Company some competition in the northern fur trade, publicity might help, and Captain Mallet agreed to finance a film-making expedition, if the resulting picture could bear the credit line "Revillon Frères presents." Unaware of this affront to all film-trade practice (the industry had long since tabooed advertising in films), Flaherty agreed and set forth. He retraced his steps through western Ungava and proceeded to reconstruct, stage, or catch on the fly a series of incidents typifying Eskimo life. Thus, in 1919 and 1920, *Nanook of the North* was made, and these are characteristic events in this first of all attempts to film from the life.

37

1920 . . . To make a long story short, I could not forget the film; I decided to go North again, this time wholly for the purpose of picturing the people I had come to like so much. Mr. John Revillon and Capt. Thierry Mallet, of Revillon Freres, undertook to finance the project. Their fur post at Cape Dufferin, on northeastern Hudson Bay, was to be the nucleus for my work.

On the 15th of August we let go anchor in the mouth of the Innusuk River, and the five gaunt and melancholy looking buildings which make up the post stood out on a boulder-ridden slope less than half a mile away.

Of the Eskimos who were known to the post, a dozen all told were selected for the film. Of these, Nanook, a character famous in the country, I chose as my chief man. Besides him, and much to his approval, I took on three younger men as helpers. This also meant their wives and families, dogs to the number of 25, sledges, kayaks, and hunting impedimenta.

The first film to be made was that of a walrus hunt. From Nanook I heard of "Walrus Island." On its south end, a surf-bound beach, there were in summer, he said, many walrus, judging from signs that had been seen by a winter sealing crowd of Eskimos who at one time had been caught there by a break-up of the ice. "The people do not go out to the island in summer," he said, "for not only is it out of sight of land, but it is ringed with heavy surf — dangerous landing for kayaks. But for a long time I have had my eye on your whaleboat, and I am sure, if the seas are smooth, it is big enough for crossing over, and just the thing for landing."

"Suppose we go," said I, "do you know that you and your men may have to give up making a kill, if it interferes with my film? Will you remember that it is the picture of you hunting the ivuik that I want, and not their meat?"

"Yes, yes, the aggie will come first," earnestly he assured me. "Not a man will stir, not a harpoon will be thrown until you give the sign. It is my word." We shook hands and agreed to start the next day.

But for three days we lay along the coast, before the big seas died down. The wind began blowing off the land. We broke out our leg o' mutton. Before the day was half done a film of gray far out in the west told us we were in sight of Walrus Island.

We looked about for a landing. Just beyond the shoulder of a little cove, "Ivuik! Ivuik!" called Nanook, and sure enough, on the gleaming black surf-worn rocks lay a great herd sprawled out asleep.

Down wind we went, careful as to muffled oars, and landed waist-deep in the surf. Nanook went off alone toward the sleeping herd; he returned, saying they were undisturbed. However, it was much too dark for pictures; we would have to wait until morning. "Yes," said Nanook, in answer to my fears, "if the wind holds in the same quarter they will not get our scent." Not daring to build a driftwood fire, we made out our evening meal on raw bacon, sea biscuit, and cold water.

As luck would have it, the wind did hold. With harpoon set and a stout seal line carefully coiled, and my motion picture camera and film retorts in hand, off we crawled for the walrus ground. The herd lay sleeping — twenty great hulks guarded by two big bulls. At about minute intervals they raised their heads over the snoring and swinishly grunting herd and slowly looked around, then sank to sleep again. Slowly I snaked up to the sheltering screen of a big boulder, and Nanook, the end of his harpoon line lashed around the boulder, snaked more slowly still out toward them. Once in the open he could move only when the sentinels dropped their heads in sleep. Hours passed, it seemed, but finally he had crawled close in. The sentinels became suspicious and stupidly stared toward him. Slowly they turned their slobbering heads to and fro; Nanook swung his own head in lugubrious unison. They rolled on their sides to scratch themselves; Nanook grotesquely did like-wise. Finally the sentinels seemed satisfied; their heads dropped in sleep once more. Now only a dozen feet intervened; quickly Nanook closed in. As I signalled he rose upon his feet, and with his harpoon held high, like lightning he struck down at the nearest bull. A bellow and a roar, and twenty great walrus rolled with incredible speed down the wave-washed slope of the rocks to the sea.

By night all my stock of film was exposed. The whaleboat was full of walrus meat and ivory. Nanook never had such walrus-hunting and never had I such filming as that on Walrus Island.

Three days later the post bell clangs out the welcome news that the kablunak is about to show his ivuik aggie. Men, old men, women, old women, boys, girls, and small children file into the factor's house. Soon there is not an inch of space to spare. The trader turns down the lamps. The projector light shoots over the shocks of heads upon the blanket which is the screen.

Then the picture. A figure appears. There is silence. They do not understand. "See, it is Nanook!" the trader cries. The Nanook in the flesh laughs his embarrassment. "Ah! Ah! Ah!" they all exclaim. Then silence. The figure moves. The silence deepens. They cannot understand. They turn their heads. They stare at the projector. They stare at its beam of magic light. They stare at Nanook, the most surprised of all, and again their heads turn toward the screen. They follow the figure which now snakes toward the background. There is something in the background. The something moves. It lifts its head.

"Ivuik! Ivuik!" shakes the room. The figure stands up, harpoon poised in hand.

"Be sure of your harpoon! Be sure of your harpoon!" the audience cries.

The figure strikes down; the walrus rolls off into the sea. More figures rush in; they grab the harpoon line. For dear life they hold on.

"Hold him! Hold him!" shout the men. "Hold him! Hold him!" squeal the women. "Hold him! Hold him!" pipe the children.

The walrus's mate dives in, and by locking tusks attempts rescue.

"Hold him!" gasps the crowd.

Nanook and his crew, although their arms seem to be breaking, hold on. But slowly and surely the threshing walrus drags the figures nearer the sea.

"Hold him! Hold him!" they despair. They are breathing hard. "Dig in! Dig in!" they rasp, as Nanook's feet slip another inch through the sand.

Deep silence. Suddenly the line sags, the crew, like a flash, draw in the slack, and inch by inch the walrus is pulled in to shore. Bedlam rocks the house.

The fame of the film spread far up and down the coast. Every

Robert Flaherty as a boy, and his family

Flaherty in the North

The North

"Their fierceness and murderous temper
is beyond telling"

"Where would we be without them?"

Waiting for the seal to rise

Nanook builds an ice window

Making *Nanook of the North*

Nanook of the North

Nanock

The grave of Nanook

strange Eskimo that came into the post Nanook brought before me and begged that he be shown the ivuik aggie.

1920 . . . One of Nanook's problems was to construct an igloo large enough for the filming of interior scenes. The average Eskimo igloo, about 12 feet in diameter, was much too small. On the dimensions I laid out for him, a diameter of 25 feet, Nanook and his companions started to build the biggest igloo of their lives. For two days they worked, the women and children helping them. Then came the hard part — to cut inserts for five large slab-ice windows without weakening the dome. They had hardly begun when the dome fell in pieces to the ground. "Never mind," said Nanook, "I can do it next time."

For two days more they worked, but again with the same result; as soon as they began setting in the ice windows their structure fell to the ground. It was a huge joke this time, and holding their sides they laughed their misfortune away. Again Nanook began on the "big aggie igloo," but this time the women and children hauled barrels of water on sledges from the waterhole and iced the walls as fast as they went up. Finally the igloo was finished and they stood eying it as satisfied as so many children over a house of blocks. The light from the ice windows proved inadequate, however, and when the interiors were finally filmed the dome's half just over the camera had to be cut away, so Nanook and his family went to sleep and awakened with all the cold out-of-doors pouring in.

To "Harry Lauder" I deputed the care of my cameras. Bringing them from the cold outside into contact with the warm air of the base often frosted them inside and out, which necessitated taking them apart and carefully drying them piece by piece. With the motion picture cameras there was no difficulty, but with my Graflex I found to my sorrow such a complication of parts that I could not get it together again. For several days its "innards" lay strewn on my work table. "Harry Lauder" finally volunteered for the task of putting them together, and through a long evening before a flickering candle with a crowd of Eskimos around ejaculating their "ayee's" and "ah's" he managed to succeed where I had failed.

41

1920 . . . We were breaking camp before the sun had cleared the horizon. The dogs fought like wolves as they wedged in through the door of the igloo we had just vacated; the crew tried vainly by grasping legs and tails to drag them out for harnessing; Nanook, his arms around the master dog, carried him bodily to the sledge. I unlimbered the Akeley, hoping to get a few feet of it all on film. But, to my dismay, as soon as I started grinding, so brittle was the film that it broke into bits, like so much wafer glass. The thermometer read 37 degrees below zero. We were up against it, since 37 below and more would be common in weeks to come.

1920 . . . At last I thought I had shot enough scenes to make the film, and we prepared to go home. To poor old Nanook the world seemed empty. He hung about my cabin, talking over films we still could make if I would only stay on for another year. He never quite understood why I should have gone to all the fuss and bother of making the "big aggie" of him — the hunting, yes — but surely everyone knew the Eskimo, and could anything be more common than dogs and sledges and snow houses? I tried to give him an idea of the big igloos the kablunaks had for show-ing films. To him, the hundred and fifty of his fellow men, as many more at Great Whale, in the distant south, and at far-off Fort Chimo, and at Cape Wolstenholme, were practically the population of the world. The kablunak's movie igloo, into which thousands came, was utterly beyond his comprehension. They were many, I used to say, as the little stones along the shore. "And will all these kablunaks see our big aggie?" he would ask. There was never need to answer, for incredulity was written large upon his face.

At last came the signal from the lookout on the hill. Within two days I was aboard and the *Annie's* nose was headed south. Nanook followed in his kayak, until the *Annie,* gathering speed, gradually drew away. I saw him turn, still waving, toward his topek, which stood out from the low, melancholy waste of shore — all that he called home!

Less than two years later, I received word by the once-a-year mail that comes out of the North that Nanook was dead. He had ventured into the interior hoping for deer. The herds did not come his way, and he starved to death. Poor old Nanook! Our "big aggie" become *Nanook of the North* has gone into most of the odd corners of the world — into the desert of the Sahara, India, Burma, Siam, where audiences must be told that white means snow; and more kablunaks than there are stones around the shore of Nanook's home have looked upon Nanook, the kindly, the brave, the simple Eskimo.

PART TWO

The South Seas

I. *MOANA*

Arduous though they were, the two years spent in the making of *Nanook of the North* must have seemed placid to Flaherty compared with what came next: the selling of the picture to the movie industry.

> When it was ready to be shown [he wrote] I started to make the rounds of the distributors in New York with the hope that one of them would be kind and give it distribution. Naturally I took it to the biggest of the distributors first — Paramount. When the film was over, they all pulled themselves together and got up in a rather dull way, I thought, and silently left the room. The manager came up to me and very kindly put his arm around my shoulders and told me that he was terribly sorry, but it was a film that just couldn't be shown to the public. He said he had tried to do such things before and they had always ended in failure. He was very sorry indeed that I had gone through all that hardship in the North only to come to such an end, but he felt he had to tell me, and that was that.
>
> So then I went to the next biggest company, First National, and they didn't even answer the phone to me after seeing the film. I think they took it as a personal affront. I had to go humbly to the projection room and ask to be allowed to take the film away.

So it went. The freebooting days of the early movie were drawing to a close in 1922. Before that time, truly experimental films were not uncommon, because nobody was really sure what a movie was, much less what the public liked about the movies. But

47

by the early twenties, the most profitable box-office formulas were becoming manifest. It had become practicable to standardize film production in anticipation of mass tastes. Distributors were no longer interested in experimenting with what they now regarded as a predictable product. Like many another outsider, Flaherty might have had to beat in vain against the closed doors and closed minds but for the accident that the Pathé Company in those days was controlled by its parent firm, the French concern of Pathé Frères. So was Revillon Frères, the sponsor of *Nanook,* and, blood being thicker than water, Pathé rather doubtfully agreed to try to distribute the film. The next move was to give it a send-off to make it stand out from the ruck.

> The problem [wrote Flaherty] was to get one of the big theatres to show it. The biggest theatre in New York at that time was the Capitol, run by the famous showman Roxy. By this time we knew very well that to show it to Roxy cold was to invite failure. What came next was the sort of thing you have to learn to do in the movie business. The sister of the publicity head of Pathé was a great friend of Roxy's. So it was arranged to show it first to her and some of her friends and tell them where to applaud through the picture, and then they would come along to the showing to Roxy in his elaborate projection room at the Capitol. We also told them never to talk directly to Roxy about the film but to talk to each other across him as if he were not in the room. Well, by the time the film was over, Roxy was tearing his hair. He used such words as "epic," "masterpiece," and the like. He booked it.

His decision awed Pathé, but with something of his own mixture of caution and gullibility the company decided to make assurance doubly sure by "tin-canning" the film — that is, by double-featuring it with Harold Lloyd's *Grandma's Boy,* which every theater in New York was scrambling for. In this inferior position, *Nanook of the North* reached the Capitol screen.

Its notices were nothing sensational. Critics today bow before the prestige of the Flaherty tradition, but then they had nothing but their own tastes to guide them, and those whose mouths were set for romantic make-believe called it a "novelty" and let it go at that. Some others cautiously opined that it was more than a novelty in the usual sense, that *Nanook of the North* was indeed something new under the sun: a dramatic and human pattern, not contrived from paint and plaster and machinery, but elicited from life itself. The picture began to gather itself a press entirely different from the trade and fan publications which attend feverishly upon the phenomena of Hollywood. Columnists and editorial writers praised it as the sort of thing people had always thought the movies ought to do, and now it was plain that they could. And, as it made its way through the theaters, it seemed to draw an unusual audience, an audience of people who didn't often go to ordinary movies but who liked adventure, or travel, or just simple beauty. Fathers and sons enjoyed seeing it together, and children in the hundreds of thousands adored Nanook as they loved no other screen figure except Chaplin. In Europe it set a remarkable pace, running for six months in London and Paris, and doing even more sensational business in Germany, Italy, and Scandinavia. The European critics were in no doubt whatever that the film was a masterpiece, a major American contribution to the arts of our time, and their audiences backed them up.

Hollywood was just then in the midst of its successful effort to penetrate and dominate foreign-film markets and, over at Paramount, Jesse L. Lasky scrutinized the European returns on *Nanook* and grew thoughtful. His company had been the first to reject the picture as unsaleable, but Lasky was not one to cling to discredited opinions. Moreover, he realized that *Nanook* was in every way a maverick, having nothing in common with the "formula" picture except that cameras recorded both on celluloid. If its success was to be repeated, Flaherty would have to be allowed to go his gait, without benefit of the advice or supervision of studio wiseacres. This might be risky, but after all *Nanook* had cost very little to make, some $55,000. Summoning its author, Lasky said:

"I want you to go off somewhere and make me another *Nanook*. Go where you will, do what you like — I'll foot the bills. The world's your oyster."

The quondam seeker of mineral deposits was startled. He thought of himself still as a professional explorer, and had not looked beyond this one film which he had made to celebrate the people he liked so much. But now, vistas opened.

I was elated. I called up Frederick O'Brien, an old friend of mine, whose book on the South Seas, *White Shadows,* was then in the heyday of its success, and told him about it. "Let's dine on it," said he. We foregathered at the Coffee House Club. Fred brought along, amongst others, George Biddle, who had recently been painting in Tahiti. "Ten years in the North! You must be fed up with it," said Fred. "Why not take the exact opposite and go to the South Seas?" A gleam came into my wife's eyes. "Could we take the children?" she asked. "Why not? It's paradise," said Fred, and he and Biddle went into rhapsodies about the islands and their people. We were spellbound.

Especially Frances Flaherty was spellbound. This adventure-anticipating young wife had had to spend nearly ten years in a placid Connecticut suburb, minding the children, while her husband finished off his mineral explorations and made and remade his film of the North. Her chance had come, and she took it.

Thus began their film-making partnership. How they worked together neither could exactly explain, but you could sense a bit of it if you watched a Flaherty scene being filmed, and something of it comes through in "production shots." In the foreground, standing beside the cameraman or at the camera himself, stood Flaherty, gesticulating, cajoling, encouraging, cursing. Somewhere off to one side there was usually a motionless figure with a light meter in one hand and a camera in the other, silently snapping her own record of the scene. Frances Flaherty says her role in their work was that of Cassandra, continually snuffing out ideas by explaining their pitfalls and impracticalities to her enthusiastic husband. Flaherty put it just the other way round. He used to say that after the excited evening discussions of the next day's work, came the cold light of morning in which all his beautiful ideas seemed crippled and dead. It was then that Frances stepped forward. True, perhaps what they had planned would not work quite as expected, but yesterday she had seen such a sight on the beach . . . or she had been talking to someone down in the village, and it seemed that the people once used to celebrate the most extraordinary ritual — hope sprang up again, ideas began to flow. Through the years this polar relationship regularized itself, after a fashion. When they arrived in the country of a prospective film, Bob would busy himself setting up shop and getting things organized, while Frances wandered off by herself with camera in hand, just as she had done in those old days in Michigan, looking for a type, or a character or landscape, which could be made part of the story they wanted to tell. Together, at night, the two of them would pore over her still pictures, shuffling them like a pack of cards, sorting and re-sorting them in search of clues to the beauty and drama their movie cameras needed. Often, on the Flaherty films, those stills were the only script they ever had.

All this was yet to be. When the Flahertys set out for Samoa, Frances was only looking forward to adventure, to beauties of which she had only dreamed, to perils which surely would be larks, and to problems which lay shrouded in the future. She knew nothing of films and film-making. Her husband had made a successful film; he would make another. She did not know that even he was yet unconscious of the reason for *Nanook's* excellence, or that together they would experience for the first time the iron discipline of all the Flaherty films: always to discover the story in the land and the people, never to fabricate, never to impose. This is her story of the making of *Moana*.

It was the cave that brought us to Safune in the first place. We were going to the glamorous South Seas to film the life of the Polynesian as he had lived it in his islands before the white man came with his strange God, his strange manners, his strange and wonderful commodities. We should go to Samoa, for of all the Polynesians the Samoans remained the finest, the most firmly rooted in their own racial traditions, the least blemished by an alien civilization. We should go to the island of Savai'i, in western Samoa, for of all the Samoans those on Savai'i retained their old ways to the highest degree. And we should go to the village of Safune on the island of Savai'i, for here we would find the first essential of our business — fresh cold water for the development of our motion picture film. The water welled up in a dark cave, believed to be the dwelling place of spirits, and the natives of Safune never ventured through its portals.

Sailing from Apia at night, we woke up to see the sun on the tops of the highest hills behind Safune. This was the place that was to be our home, we reflected, for a year or more. Had anyone told us then that it would be two years before we would return to civilization, we should have laughed or cried, I do not know which.

The people we met when we arrived were like creatures of another time. We remembered the words of Henry Adams, friend of Stevenson, who with John LaFarge the painter, lived in Samoa in the eighteen-nineties: "It is a deep wonder to me that I have not been told that here is rustic Greece of the Golden Age, still alive, still to be looked at."

The villagers lived in about a hundred houses, which served mostly as shelters against tropical storms, since life was actually lived out of doors, on the beaches, in the clement sea that was as warm as the air, and in the palm jungles, where lurked no dangerous beasts except the wild boar, who kept to himself if left to himself. Here men and women played through the long days like children. Time had no meaning. Life was a game, a dance, a frieze on a Grecian urn.

When we first arrived in Safune, we had a meeting with the chiefs. It was held in the village guest house and there must have been twenty-five chiefs, all belonging to Safune, gathered to do us honor. We explained why we had come to Samoa and spoke of our admiration for the Samoan people and their customs. In reply, the chiefs told us how glad they were to have us come to their village. They thanked God we had come safely, expressed the hope that everything would prosper between us and them, and promised to take every possible care of us. Afterward there was a great feast.

Samoan food is delicious. Thus, from my diary: "Out of the fronds of a tall palm, coconuts are falling, where Fasitalo, 'Piece of Taro,' is cutting them down for drinking. Pretty soon he will come sliding down and tear off the green husk on a sharpened stick thrust into the ground and with his knife neatly crack the brown shell off one end — and there will be a goblet lined with the purest white, brimful of a delicious water — slightly sweet and with a slight tang — cold and clear. It is the nearest thing to nectar." In the little shed that serves the Samoan for a kitchen a great lot of stones would be heated for the roasting of the bread-fruit. On these the soft white chunks would be laid, with more hot stones over them. And coconut shells were set there, too, filled with white cream pressed from the coconut meat and covered with banana leaves, through which the steam would rise. Two hours later we would be presented with roasted fruit and a cup of coconut custard most delicately flavored, food for an epicure. In the very flavor and texture of it on my tongue, I tasted a refinement and delicacy such as I think to be the hidden spirit of a Japanese tea ceremony.

When, later, we filmed Samoan eating and drinking, we thought people would go crazy over these scenes, not only because of the appetizing look of the food but also because of the beauty and civilization of the ritual of serving. But people in New York seemed to find these eating scenes merely a boring interruption of the narrative, and we decided that their charm lay entirely in our eyes, that the camera couldn't capture it. Years later — I think it

53

was in 1937 — when Jean Renoir and a group of French film-makers gave us an *homage* in Paris, *Moana* was revived for the occasion. When the scenes of food-preparation and serving came on, all through the darkened theatre we heard a murmur of "ohs" and "ahs" and "par exemples!" The French understood!

Our big idea, of course, was that we should make a film after the pattern of *Nanook of the North*. We should find a man like Nanook, the Eskimo, a sturdy, dignified chief and head of a family, and then build our picture around him, substituting the dangers of the sea, here in the South Pacific, for those of snow and ice in the North. We would present the drama of Samoan life as it unrolled itself naturally before us, as far as possible untouched by the hand of the trader, the missionary, and the government. We began by trying to tell the Polynesians in a booklet about the Eskimos and the purpose behind the filming of *Nanook*.

When our words came back to us, retranslated from the Samoan, they had a strange new flavor. "This picture," the account ran, "tells the story of the conduct and daily lives of the Eskimo people who live in a country where the water is frozen and covered with snow, near to the North Pole, as our own country is near to the equator. That country has no trees, no fruits or eatable plants. The animals which creep on the frozen sea, these the people kill every day to keep them alive.

"This chief, Mr. Flaherty, lived with Eskimos and imitated their customs and their conduct and dressed in their kind of clothes, made of the skin of the great white quadruped known as the bear of the North Pole. He made this picture because love overflowed in his heart for the people of this country, on account of their kindliness and their bravery, and also on account of their receiving him well, and because they look very happy every day of their lives, in a life most difficult to live in the whole world.

"The high chiefs in New York, the big village in America, they saw that Mr. Flaherty had made a very useful thing; so they gathered together in council and expressed themselves like this: 'Such pictures as this will create love and friendship among all the people of the world. Then misunderstanding and quarrels will end.'

"Then the council of high chiefs in New York prepared a great feast for Mr. Flaherty and told him to make a picture like the picture of the story of Nanook. And so Mr. Flaherty has come here to Samoa to find the genuine descendants of the pure Polynesian race of ancient times, and also their good customs, as they were in the days before the missionaries and traders came to spread their customs in Samoa."

When we showed the Safune people the film of Nanook, however, on the screen hung out under the coconut trees, it made little impression on them. They were delighted to see something Lopati, as they called Bob, had made — that and nothing more. I do not believe they had any sense of importance that we wanted to make a film of them, too, for the benefit of some far-away country.

But one day two of the Safune chiefs brought a chief from Vaisala to call on us. One of the two from Safune, a great missionary chief, came in his white shirt and coat. It was very hot, but this was his idea of what we, the white people, wanted. Oh, the heart-rending difficulty of getting behind the past hundred years, behind the missionary, the trader and the government — even here in Safune — and seeing the Samoan as he really was! The other two chiefs were dressed in their Samoan ulas, necklaces of flowers, and siapos, or bark-cloth lava-lavas. We told them how very much we liked their own clothes. They listened with the closest attention. It seemed to be a new idea to them that neither Christ nor we, the papalangi, really wished to see them in the white man's clothes. Through the influence of the missionary it had come about that the Samoan who had only a siapo was looked down upon. The visiting chief now said that he would order all his village, men, women, and children, henceforth to wear only siapos.

With such understandings established, we were ready to start work. As we always did afterward, we began by trying to explore the life of the people, to penetrate to the things that gave life meaning for them. The best way to do this is to start with very simple, everyday things and let them lead you toward the feelings and beliefs which lie at the core of every people's life. We learned later that this is an absolutely necessary part of the process of getting close to our subject, but in this first joint attempt we were shaken by doubts. Enchanted though we were by everything we were seeing and filming, much of it seemed to us trivial, unrelated, lacking in pattern. Still, nothing to do but get on with it . . .

As nearly always happened, many of our best sequences came to us by accident. Among the villagers who came to visit us in the early days, for one reason or another, or no reason at all, was Tu'ungaita. She had a reason. She had come to offer for sale the beautiful baskets that she made out of sun-dried strips of pandanus leaf. I thought I should like the children to learn how to make baskets, too, and I asked Tu'ungaita to come and stay with us. She was skilled in another art besides basketry, the making of tapa, the chief art of the women of Samoa. Nowadays most of the printed cloth for the lava-lavas worn by both men and women comes from Apia — and before that from Manchester, Liverpool, and Edinburgh — or perhaps from Japan. In old days the garments were made from bark-cloth beaten out of strips of the paper-mulberry. You still see plenty of siapos, or bark-cloth lava-lavas in Samoa, but they belong to a vanishing order.

Tu'ungaita used to sit in the shade of a big mango-tree near the house and cut the strips of inner white bark from the mulberry branches. These she would moisten with water, paste on a flat board, and scrape clean with a clam shell. Then she would roll them up as you might a ribbon to pound them out on the board, one at a time, with a corrugated wooden mallet. Slowly, incredibly, the strips widened from three or four inches to as many feet, and became gossamer sheets of beautiful cloth. Someone would sit beside her and patch the inevitable holes with bits of tapa stuck down with raw arrow-root. Next a kind of stencil, or block for printing, would be made by sewing together several wide strips of pandanus and making a raised design on this, in straight lines, of the spines of coconut leaves and fibers from the husks. Over this Tu'ungaita would lay her sheets of tapa and with a tapa-brush dipped in a coconut shell paint-pot rub the design off on the cloth. The color used is invariably a red stain that comes from the seeds of the sandalwood. Another kind of tapa is not stencilled at all, but is painted, generally in three colors —

black from the candlenut, yellow from turmeric, and red from sandalwood seeds.

In all these processes Tu'ungaita excelled, and, when she got out her tapa-mallet, she always drew around her an admiring group of younger women and girls, including her small grand-daughter, who sat fascinated, watching her by the hour. For the mother of our Samoan family, who could possibly be better than Tu'ungaita, with her gentle ways and quiet efficiency?

Each day the sun shone brighter and brighter as it rolled along its heavenly arc, and the reef glittered more blindingly. The trades blew soft by day and cool by night, and the moon waxed and waned and shed white radiance through the shimmering palms. Here we were — tropic sun and moon, palms, everything as advertised; the victrola playing, the cook cooking, the electric lights lighting, the fans fanning, and only the reels remaining to be reeled. But June, July, and August drifted by — August, September, and October — and we had not made an inch of permanent film.

All this time, besides settling and working out the technical problems of our photography, we were looking for our characters. It was no easy task to find them. Strange as it may seem, types that photograph well are few. In these equatorial latitudes of lotus ease, thought has molded the faces not deeply if at all, and in repose they become curiously empty. So we roamed the neighboring villages and invited in any and every person that looked at all possible and we studied and made tests and studied again. It was all rather discouraging and bare of results in those first months of our stay in the village of Safune, on the island of Savai'i, in far-away Samoa.

The traditional romance of the Pacific islands is bound up with the animal life of the sea. The natives are children of the sea. Familiar enough in the West are the stories of their wonderful skill and fearlessness as divers, as swimmers, as fishermen. As common as the day to them are the creatures of the underwater world. To us they are strange and terrifying, but, particularly if huge, none the less fascinating. Everybody loves to see them on the screen; everybody loves the sport of a good hunt for them and a fair fight. The first thing we had to do, once we were settled in Samoa, was to look for this type of 100% screen material.

From white old-timers we eagerly questioned at the beginning, we received little comfort. One by one our list of hopes — sharks, octopuses, robber-crabs — they negatived. A big octopus they had never seen — did not believe it existed, certainly not in Samoa. "Wait," said Bob to me, nothing daunted. He had had a similar experience among the Eskimos; one need not expect these aliens to know anything of the country except their own particular business in it. "Wait and question the natives, you will see."

I well remember a day — the chiefs of Safune had given us a great feast — when a "traveling," a malanga, was passing through Safune from villages down the coast. A large octopus had been seen, some of the visiting chiefs announced, in the passage of the reef at Satawa. "I told you so!" exulted Bob. How big was it? It was big, they said, "Tele lava," its body was as big as that house over there. Incredible! And yet, why not? Larger than the largest known whale was the carcass of an octopus found off the coast of Madagascar. Where there were little ones, was it not reasonable to expect to find big ones? Besides, in the deep-water reef of Asau, which was on the way to Satawa, we had heard there were tiger-sharks. We prepared forthwith to make a great malanga of our own down the coast to Asau and Satawa and sent word ahead of our coming.

The news spreads fast. In the guest-house of Asau all the chiefs, like statues in bronze, are waiting to receive us. They are seated cross-legged on mats spread on the floor. The air is heavy and sweet with the ceremonial oil with which their bodies glisten and with the musky fragrance of the waxlike flower-chains and chaplets that they wear. The highest chief holds in his hand a kava root, like a knotted, gnarled club; as we take our places, he tosses it on the mat before us. In language sacred to his rank he begins the speech of welcome. How glad they are to see us! The bronze, beflowered heads nod and warm the speaker to his theme.

And now the taupou, the principal village maiden, comes in and seats herself before the kava-bowl. The root has been pounded to dust, the dust put into the bowl and water from a coconut shell bottle poured upon it. With movements as beautiful as the movements of a dance, she sweeps the bowl with golden strands of bark and squeezes and wrings out the juices of the powdered root. Every movement must be exact and according to the set form of this ritual, which is as ancient as the race itself. She holds the drenched strands up and watches the yellowing liquid stream. Clap the hands, you that sit beside the bowl, and call the names of guests and chiefs, the rank of each, and make no blunder in the order of their drinking; for from a breach of precedence like that wars have been known to spring. Holding high the polished half-shell of the cup, thrice-filled, the talking-chief stands before the guest. With a sweep of the arm and hand that holds the cup, bending low, he presents it. When at last all the speeches are done, it is time — finally — for talk of octopuses and sharks and the drama of the sea.

Yes, they are willing to do everything the millionaire asks. Bob, alas, had acquired the name of "The Millionaire" long before we landed in Safune. All our goods that had come on before us had been marked with high insurance values. Of course the half-castes saw those figures on the boxes and drew their own conclusions. We were millionaires, and there you are. The report spread over the island like wild-fire. We never outlived it, and we had to live up to it all the time we remained in Samoa.

Yes, yes, they will do whatever the millionaire wants. They will entice the sharks to shore with bait. Early morning is the best time. They will be ready with their iron-pointed spears. But meanwhile they have prepared a dance for the papalangi, the white people of strange whims. Many pigs have been killed, and pigeons and fish, many taros baked. Why should the white man bother about the doubtful, useless hunting of the sea creatures when the greatest honors that Samoa can offer are prepared for him?

And so it happens that at the appointed hour the village is suddenly alive with a gathering of all the people, each one bedecked with the brilliant red and white and green of flowers and leaves, threaded and twined and woven in patterned chains and wreaths, necklaces of buds, fillets of delicate petals. The drum

59

beats. The ranks of the young men have formed. In short sallies they advance, falling on one knee, spring up and advancing again with a tinkling of anklet shells. Finally they are before us, and the charm of the perfect rhythm of the mass has become the charm of individual movement. The face of the young chief, so finely chiseled and so like a mask — it has come alive, it is shining. And the watchers! Unconsciously they slip into the rhythm, bodies swaying, hands clapping, lips moving to the song. A ceremonial dance-knife slips. "Ai! Ai!" As with one voice, a derisive shout breaks out from the keenest, most critical audience in the world. For is it not the time when the people of Asau must prove themselves the best dancers on Savai'i? Tomorrow, perhaps, the papalangi will go to Vaisala. And the day after that they will be in Satawa, that proud and foolish village that claims for itself the greatest feats of dancing. Let there be no blunders then.

Slowly, next day, we chug out over the placid harbor with a last lingering look toward the abandoned palm shelter where, through the long morning, hunters of the shark waited in vain while their bait lay untouched on the rocks.

Nine dances at Asau! Vaisala claimed us next. And again the kava root was tossed upon the mat. The kava flowed, the drum beat and the dancing began. Came darkness and still there was no abatement. What should we do? We were on a business trip. We had a film to make. We had to see sharks and octopuses, and not dances. What could we do with dances? Here we were, wasting all our precious time, our precious money, all our resources. Desperately we took counsel. No more sivas! We coached our talking-chief. Tomorrow with the chiefs of Satawa he must be kind but firm. Positively no sivas. He promised he would do his best.

Speak he did; and anxiously we watched the chiefs of Satawa as they followed his words. We saw how their eyes fell and we noted the rueful smile that spread over their faces — they, the best dancers of Savai'i! Our talking-chief looked at us, and we looked at one another — criminals, caught in the act. Very well, then; one siva, only one — or, at most, two, no more.

And what about the octopus? — Early in the morning — it is

60

the best time — they will go to the place where the big fe'e is some-times seen. They show us the bait, a mottled shell that gives the appearance of a shell-fish. This they will dangle like a choice tidbit at the door of the murky cave where the octopus lies in wait for its prey.

And yet, next morning, each house has its group of garland-makers and its fragrant heaps of frangipani, hibiscus, banana buds, and shining leaves. Siva! Siva! "The Millionaire!" Ah, now he would see. Asau, Vaisala — poof! Now he would see them at Satawa — the best dancers of all!

Through the blur of that afternoon, dancing arms and dancing feet faded in and out, in and out of my benumbed consciousness. I could see nothing but a woman, seemingly half-witted, with half-witted grin, who insisted upon keeping herself exactly in the eye of Bob's camera. "Get her, get her!" I almost screamed at him. "Get her just like that and we'll go back to New York!"

When finally the flood of dances was exhausted and there was nobody left in all Satawa to dance for us, our talking-chief — the octopus long since forgotten — thanked our hosts — "Ah, lelei, le siva, lelei" — "Ah, how fine the siva, how fine." But alas for our animal sequences. Alas for our drama of the sea. Alas for our poor film of Samoan life. We returned from our malanga without one additional foot of negative.

It was too much. We sank into a state of confirmed pessimism. These people were not fishers, not hunters. Why not acknowledge the fact once for all?

We knew that our white compatriots could not see any film material in the people and their simple lives. The Samoans were neither interesting nor attractive to them. What did we think we could find in them? And, God help us, through the blackest months that ever darkened our lives, we tortured ourselves with the same question.

Unfortunately we had come to Samoa with preconceived no-tions about the element of struggle necessary for a film. We did not have any scenario, but we had the idea that we were going to make just such another film as *Nanook*, with the drama of strug-gle to be found in the element of the sea.

Here was the hitch, however. In the North the whole of life is a very grim affair, an endless struggle for existence. Not only that, but the drama is one of action that we understand because it comes close to our own lives and the eternal competition for daily bread. In the South there is no struggle for existence. The mere getting of food is as incidental as a game. The environment is perfect as it is. It has never demanded of the people the development of any intellectual life, any ingenuity, any adaptation to change. Drama exists, but it is a very subtle thing, quite apart from anything we understand. It is to be found in nothing more nor less than custom — fa'a Samoa. Therein the people build their whole lives. If you break fa'a Samoa, you break their lives to pieces and they die.

As we realized the problem we were facing, black despair settled over every one of us. We could not make a picture out of heroic things the people did not really do. As for fa'a Samoa, that was something psychological. It expressed itself in mass ceremonies, in set forms and endless dances, and particularly simply in talking. How in heaven's name are you going to get a picture out of that? How are you going to photograph talk? The only thing we could do, as we saw it, was just to make the best of a very bad business and get home as soon as possible.

That we did, in the end, get something else came about through bungling and accident and a happy technical discovery. When we projected our first experiments on the screen, the people came out a dirty black, and there was nothing attractive about them at all. The orthochromatic film we were using did not give the proper-color value to their beautiful light brown skin. An orthochromatic film takes red as black, and wherever red enters into a color, it is seriously distorted. We had brought with us a color camera, however, with the idea of making some experiments in motion picture color-work. In color-photography, panchromatic film is used — a color-corrected film, sensitive to red. It was an experimental use of this film with our ordinary black-and-white camera that threw the first gleam of light on our difficulty. We found that the panchromatic film, used in direct sunlight, gave an extraordinary stereoscopic effect. The figures jumped right out of the screen. They had roundness and modeling and looked alive and, because of the color correction, retained their full beauty of texture. The setting immediately acquired a new significance. There are a hundred different tones of green in a tropical island — the dark, shiny green of the breadfruit, the sage-green of the taro, the clear brilliant green of the coconuts. With the orthochromatic film, green, like red, is always dark. Our new process gave the proper color-value to each leaf. We could make even a fish look interesting because it was as beautiful in the photograph as it was in reality.

In the past, photographers had made use of panchromatic film for outdoor shots, particularly for cloud effects, but sparingly. It required an entirely different technique in the laboratory. In an ordinary laboratory a red light was considered safe, because the orthochromatic film was not sensitive to red. Panchromatic film had to be developed in absolute darkness. The obvious difficulty of handling it in the laboratory was one reason why it had been so little used up to that time.

At last we had the solution of our problem. The drama of our picture should lie in its sheer beauty, the beauty of fa'a Samoa, rendered by panchromatic film.

The old primitive Polynesian life was changing, changing so rapidly that already one had a sense of the end, of hurry to catch it as it went — as a matter of fact, we had come only just in time to see a fleeting ghost. The Polynesia we pictured must necessarily be "Christianized" since Christianity had taken firm root among the islands. But though the missionaries clipped the shoulder-length hair of the Polynesian and changed his loin-cloth from grass to print — changed him outwardly — at heart he remained very much as he had been. When they found him, he was more Christian than themselves. He welcomed them with more brotherly love than the missionaries among themselves ever dreamed of. He took their songs and enriched them with his own fine gift of music and its perfect expression in community singing. He took their ritual and incorporated it in the still more beautiful and ordered ritual of his own daily life. He took the gospel of giving and outdid the perfect parable of the widow's mite; for he makes a festival of giving and sharing — they are his joy. He adopted as an emblem of Godliness the coat, collar, and tie — God save the mark! They were to him but another symbol of his own instinctive love of the decorous, expressed so beautifully in his own native fashion.

The true Samoan does not know the meaning of private property; he does not know the meaning of gain. He does not know want nor the fear of poverty. If his house burns down, there is always his neighbor's house. If he gets no fish, there are always his neighbor's fish. Small wonder his inclination is for singing and dancing, for flowers and loving. Wherever he walks, it is "Malie, malie!" — "Beautiful, beautiful!"

In some ways the Samoans are curiously like us. Physically I have no sense of difference, color notwithstanding. There was not a facial type among them that I could not recognize as familiar — but for the expression of the eyes. There was the difference, the gulf, the chasm. These people have no thought-life, no intellect. They have not tasted of the Tree of Knowledge. Existence for them is a beautiful plain, sun-blessed, fertile, flower-spread, balm-kissed, a plain where life runs in and out and in and out like an unending repetition of song. Why, their singing is the very epitome of their life, never in solo, ever in chorus, instinct with a harmony and a rhythm as absolute as nature herself and as unemotional.

They mate as the birds mate, for the purpose and period of reproduction. Under their social system, in which every child is a welcome pair of hands for planting taro, for spearing fish, for weaving mats, there is no denial of motherhood; the love and bearing of children is whole-souled and free. The first cry of a newborn child is heralded by a shout that echoes through the whole village. The families meet for mutual congratulation with an exchange of mats and presents. The man, following his instincts, later on may take another wife; the woman, following hers, will go back to her father's house and in peace and dignity unhampered and the fullness of her strength rear her young. Nature, satisfied, takes no toll in "problems."

We were making a film of this wonderful life so different from our own. We had tried to mold it into a dramatic form, a form of struggle and danger, into which it fitted not at all. Our spirits were worn out with the struggle we had made; and they were bowing down and worshipping and weeping with the beauty of these people and our love for them. Could any of this that we felt, be translated into terms of motion for the screen? That thing typical of their lives in which there was the most expression through action was the siva, the dance. We had tried to film the dance before. We had tried with orthochromatic film and our disgust with the results had put the siva as a screen possibility far from our minds. But now, with panchromatic film to work with, we had a whole new palette for our brush. We wrote out a siva sequence. We had come to know the siva as the people themselves felt about it, and it was this, and not merely its outward form, that we wanted to portray.

And so we filmed the little sequence — all in the hottest heat of the hot season, perspiration pouring off us in bucketfuls, the rubber gaskets melting out of the cameras. And what was the result? It was *good*, beyond all expectation good. Never had Ta'avale danced like that before, and blessed be panchromatic film and sunlight. He and Fa'angase stood out from the screen bodily. They were living and beautiful and dramatic. We looked at one another, hardly believing. We were confused. It was beyond us, something outside of ourselves. Was it really to be for us to portray the beauty of these people? Had we only to flash picture after picture like this — just a simple "Here they are; here they are in the commonest affairs of their nature-blessed untroubled lives; see how lovely, how gracious, a vision of ancient Greece"?

And yet, how did we know? How could we tell? Little devils of doubt crept into our minds. How could we be the judges in the motion picture world any more? We knew these people now; we had drunk deep of their life. We had become one with them. The siva was as thrilling to us as if we had been native born. I had seen the fathers and mothers of Samoa watching their children in the dance. How they watched, how they coached, how their eyes sparkled, how they smiled their heart-bursting pride! Now my own children danced the siva. They put on their beads and flowers, oiled themselves, and marched over to dance before all the people. The children loved it and the dear people laughed. And I — was I proud!

Just when we had begun to hope that we had solved our problems, disaster struck us.

Here we were, after a year's work in Samoa, face to face with

the most cruel thing that could possibly have happened to us —
a flaw in our negative. Faint but unmistakable, at regular intervals, were dark flashes on the film.

We made experiments innumerable. Nothing we could think of
was too far-fetched or too obvious, too simple or too complicated,
to try and try again. Night after night I sat up alone until cock-
crow, my lamp the single spot of light in the village of dark fales
and darker bush, waiting for Bob to bring the final test from the
laboratory. June, July, week after week, day and night and night
and day, we worked, and always the result was the same — always
the test showed the same baffling waver.

Beside the cave in which we developed our film was another
one, bigger and more open. As an experiment we washed a test
in this second cave, and the strip of negative showed no queer
streaks or waver. Was there, then, something the matter with the
clean, clear, perfect water of our cave? We tore up the platform
that had been put down in the cave. Bob pointed to a white deposit
on the rocks on the bottom of the pool. From the washing of the
negative after developing, a deposit of silver nitrate had formed
in the pool. The water had not flushed it out, as we had supposed,
with the regular rising and falling of the tides. Our fresh negative,
washed in water chemically tainted with nitrate, had been regu-
larly retoned with disastrous results.

Now much was clear to us besides the fearful difficulty with
the film. Bob had been drinking the cave water. The *Encyclopaedia* gave the symptoms of nitrate poisoning. They were exactly the
symptoms of the strange illness that had overtaken Bob in Tufu,
when we were on our malanga in search of animal and sea sequences.

It was on a Tuesday morning that he was taken sick. We des-
patched a messenger from Tufu to the German trader at Safune,
to send a boat, but it could not reach Falealupo, the nearest point
of call, before Saturday. Bob was not able to touch food and grew
very weak. All he took was an opiate to ease the pain a little.
I simply sat and awaited the signal for another dose when the pain
became too bad.

Everybody in Tufu was most kind and thoughtful. The inspector called every day, and the priests and the traders, and twice
a day came the village, with its pigs and baskets of food. The

villagers always came in a body, each walking slowly with head bent and a hand behind the back, and their talking-man invariably made some graceful little speech.

Five days dragged by. The boat was due from Safune, and the time had arrived for Bob to be moved to Falealupo. He would have to be carried on a stretcher, of course. I spoke about it to Ta'avale, who was playing our Moana. He seemed unusually moved and troubled. I knew at once that it was something fa'a Samoa again; I had developed a nose like a hound for that sort of thing. It was about carrying Mr. Flaherty to Falealupo. It was all right, except that Mr. Flaherty would have to walk . . . at the other end of the village . . . a little way. Fantastic! But it could not be helped. That spectral, vaporish place where the swamp comes in, where the wind goes mad and the pathway is choked with coconuts and giant leaves, bristling and keen-edged as blades — a spirit dwells there. Had I not seen him myself, leaping in the treetops and grinning down? I pulled myself together. "Do you mean to tell me you believe such nonsense?" I said severely. But Ta'avale was no whit abashed. "Alofa tele Lopati," he insisted, repeating it over and over. "We love Lopati too much!" Many people had died at that spot, carried past in just that way. But there was safety in walking. Please, please! "Alofa tele Lopati!" Ta'avale was almost in tears.

Now came all the chiefs of Tufu into the house to say goodbye. Bob lay helpless behind the tapa curtain. Fialelei sat by me and translated. The talking-chief looked first at her and then at me. I cannot tell you now the words he spoke, but — phrase by phrase, with pauses while Fialelei would tell me what he said, measured, like music — simply, oh, so very simply, with dignity and beauty he spoke, in a manner that filled me with deep wonder, the deepest and truest things we know of comfort and of love. "Who are these people?" I cried within myself. "Who are you! Who are you!"

Then, led by a native missionary, we set out on our way to Falealupo, Bob under a white sheet on a litter borne on the shoulders of the chiefs of Tufu. At the place of the spirit the missionary faced about and raised his hand. The litter was lowered and Bob walked.

Once again in Falealupo, we made our way into the big windy

fale of our English host. Through the gray hours of waiting, there was the inspector, kindness itself. And there were an old captain and a Catholic missionary whom the natives wanted to burn. "Give them tea," Bob would call out. "Stay to luncheon. Get the cigars — some cigarettes! Have you matches? Sit down, sit down, you don't have to go." And I poured and passed and passed and poured and gave Bob his opiate and chatted and laughed and clutched my agony of fear to myself.

"O le va'a!" somebody cried. On to the strip of sea framed between the pillars of the fale slipped the black nose of the steamer. I choked out the news to Bob and rushed behind the curtain and into Fialelei's arms and Fa'angase's and cried and cried, the two of them crying with me.

Dr. Ritchie, who had come on the boat, took Bob to Apia, dropping me off at Safune, where the children had remained under the care of Annie, our Irish nurse. Every day or every other day I had news by wireless, but the days crept by slowly. A spirit was gone and the house was empty.

Then at last came a wireless message to have a boat waiting outside the reef at midnight. It was moonlight again, just a month since our moonlight nights at Tufu. While I waited, I fell asleep and dreamed that he came up on the veranda and took me in his arms and that I could feel every bone in his body, but . . . I could have laughed or cried . . . he smiled down at me. There were the piano and the violin. "Shall we play a little?" he said.

It was just twelve when I awoke. I opened up the kitchen — he would want coffee — and set places at the table. Finally came the whistle of a boat far out and the call of the bugle from shore. Then a long wait — and then the bugle, coming nearer and again nearer and nearer, theatrically. Rain fell down, splashing in the night. Came a glimmering up the path — the white figure would be his — and now they were bringing him up on the veranda. He sank into his chair. Seeing him, I could not speak. I brought the coffee, but he left it barely tasted. One by one, the household slipped away. The next day Bauer, the trader, came to see him. He stared. "My Gott!" he cried.

Nevertheless we pitched right into filming. Never did we have

such a week: up at the first flush of dawn; picturing morning and
night; working like demons. The mere sight of Bob had stirred
the whole village to life again. With pity in their eyes as they
looked at him, they kept repeating, "Alofa, alofa, alofa" —
"Love, love, love."

Our lives saved, the picture saved, everything saved, now at last
we could make a beginning of the end. We had determined that
we would make our picture simply of things fa'a Samoa — of the
everyday life of the village. Only one important scene remained
to be made, the climax of the film in our eyes — the tattooing
of Ta'avale. The old tufunga, tattooer, of the village became a
member of the cast early in the year. He was a dear old man,
just the type for the part. His is an art that has come down to
him from his forefathers. The tufunga is a great chief and tattooing is a very expensive affair, attended with great ceremony. To
the Samoan man, it is the crucial event in a lifetime, from which
all other happenings are dated. Until he is tattooed, no matter
how old he may be, the Samoan man is still considered and treated
as a boy.

We had seen two persons tattooed. The process is very painful.
Needle points of bone — like a fine-toothed comb, impregnated
with dye — bite into the skin under the tap-tap of the hammer.
The skin is held taut and the surplus dye and blood are wiped
away as the needles tap along the line marked out for the pattern.
The whole pattern, like breeches of fine blue silk, extends from
above the waist to below the knee, solidly. But only a little tattooing is done at one time, the amount depending on the strength
of the subject.

Tattooing is the beautification of the body by a race who, without metals, without clay, express their feeling for beauty in the
perfection of their own glorious bodies. Deeper than that, however, is its spring in a common human need, the need for struggle,
for some test of endurance, some supreme mark of individual
worth and proof of the quality of the man. The Eskimo has struggle thrust upon him — he could not escape it if he would. He
meets it like a man and we admire him. In Polynesia, what is it
that can keep alive the spirit of man but his own respect for what

69

he is — the God that is within him? And so it is that tattooing stands for valor and courage and all those qualities in which a man takes pride.

Would Ta'avale go through with it for us — for the film? If ever there was a young god physically, it was Ta'avale. But Ta'avale was human, too, and he did dread the ordeal. Once started, he would have to go on with it — six weeks of torture and two weeks more of a crippled body! Many Samoan boys are not tattooed these days because the missionaries discourage tattooing. It was really hard for Ta'avale to decide. But at last the plunge was taken. He would follow the tradition of his race.

There he lay one day, flat on his stomach on the floor, surrounded by his gentle and sympathetic and admiring friends — all the members of our movie family. The tufunga plied his hammer and the needles bit sharp into the flesh. There was pain in the clenched hands stretched out on the matting. Ta'avale's face when he looked up was twisted and pale, but in it was no thought of flinching. It was not only his own pride that was at stake but the honor of all Samoa. And faithfully the camera made its record of a ceremonial that like so much else in the South Seas was destined soon to pass before an inrushing tide of alien civilization.

When he was not under the tufunga's hands, Ta'avale went about singing and laughing like a youngster with his first long trousers. He would pull his lava-lava down from his back and show us the fine pattern and remark on how beautifully it was done. His joy and pride knew no bounds. He was certainly the hero of the film now. None of the others had done so much as this. He was the sole object of the entire attention and solicitude of us all.

The time came at last for us to say goodbye to Safune. Our work was done. There was no possible excuse for lingering longer. Of the parting, however, I cannot write . . . Within eight hours we were in Apia, just in time for a Sunday tea-party at one of the government plantations — tea and tennis! There were the children in their Sunday bibs and tuckers playing sweetly with the

70

other little children in their Sunday bibs and tuckers. Tea and tennis! How vastly simple, how overwhelmingly sane! . . . Already Safune was a thousand miles away — unheard of, insubstantial, incredible creation of incredible imagination, figment of a dream.

II. *TABU*

"You have no protagonist, nor have you betrayed us with a falsified story — instead, with the unerring instinct of the artist, you have weaved a pattern from Nature herself, from sky, clouds, water, trees, hills and the everyday simple acts of men, women, and children.

"Theocritus did no more. He took the sky and clouds, trees, shepherds and maidens, and sang of goats and swineherds, and the hills of his beloved Sicily. Heaven knows I don't want to be fulsome, but as I told them last night, and they afterwards agreed with me, *Moana* reaches the dignity of an epic poem, and will always be a classic in the hearts of those who see it."

Thus wrote Austin Strong, Stevenson's son-in-law, in a letter to Flaherty which was nothing if not fulsome. Laurence Stallings said in the *World,* "The Samoan picture is not based upon 'The Golden Bough.' It is 'The Golden Bough.' I do not think a picture can be greater than this Samoan epic. It hangs together with an eternal grace."

"It has within it the soul of an admirable race," wrote Robert Sherwood, and prediction was widespread that, once the picture was generally shown, steamship offices would be swamped by people wanting to go to Samoa. For, said Matthew Josephson, "Flaherty has done more than give us only a beautiful spectacle. With his broad vision he has suddenly made us think seriously, in between the Florida boom and our hunting for bread and butter

71

in Wall Street, about the art of life. Here, he says to us, are people who are *successful in the art of life.* Are we that, with our motor-cars, factories, sky-scrapers, radio-receivers?" Tributes such as these did much to dispel the doubts which gnawed the Flahertys in those last months in Safune, when they feared that they had come too close to their subject to project it to anyone else. At that, there was an occasional note of doubt mingled with the hosannahs the picture evoked. Those who were eager to leave the America of 1926 and get back to Eden by the first boat were thus admonished by Robert Littell in *The New Republic:*

"This little paradise where suffering has to be kept artificially alive, where food is given without work, fills us with fallacious envy. Set us all down in the land of Mr. Flaherty's Moana under a palm tree, and we would for a while be happy, lazy in the sun, re-joicing in simplicity, paradise regained. But after a while the sea and the sun and the perpetual free-lunch would pall, and there would creep into our lives, one by one, all the familiar faces we had cursed and left behind forever; bold fillings and carbon copies, letters of condolence and general conversation, poker debts and the League of Nations, Methodists, mortgages, and Something on the Hip, flypaper, Chambers of Commerce and Ph.D. degrees, the sum total of which, curiously enough, goes by the name of civilization."

Mr. Littell said further: "The Heaven in the South Seas which the white man thought he had discovered for himself is not for him at all. It might have lasted for the native. In a very few corners some traces of it may still be found. Whether Mr. Flaherty found one of these corners intact, or whether he welded traces of the real thing with his imagination of it does not matter. His reconstruction remains a living reconstruction." That this was sound analysis is evidenced by the verdict of the only possible judges of the matter, a group of Samoan chiefs who were brought to Apia to see *Moana.* "To them," wrote C. E. Hall to Flaherty, "the film pos-

"Here is rustic Greece of the Golden Age,

"still alive, still to be looked at"

"Through the blur of that afternoon, dancing arms and dancing feet
faded in and out of our benumbed consciousness"

"Get her, get her! Get her just like that and we'll go back to New York!"

"When we took our first shots, the people came out a dirty black, and there was nothing attractive about them at all"

"But on panchromatic film, the figures jumped right out of the screen. They had roundness and modeling and looked alive"

"Every movement must be exact and according to the set form of the ritual, which is as ancient as the race itself"

Fa'a Samoa

"Bob under a white sheet on a litter, borne on the shoulders of the chiefs of Tufu"

Tattooing

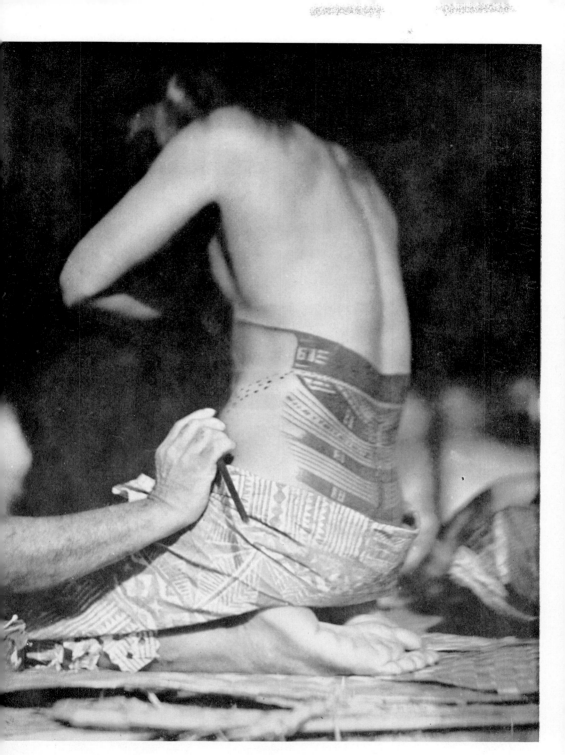

"Like breeches of fine blue silk"

"Unheard-of, insubstantial, incredible creation of incredible imagination, figment of a dream"

Tabu

Moana

Robert Flaherty and F. W. Murnau aboard their yacht, the *Moana*

sessed no new beauty. They watched silently the feats of climbing, swimming, pig-hunting, and canoe adventures as commonplace events in the old Samoan life. But they missed nothing of the scarcely perceptible gesture and detail of ceremony so full of significance to them.

"The picture faded from the sheet, and they turned sadly away, knowing full well that never again would these things be.

"To my inquiries, the picture was 'lelei lava' (good exceedingly). Their only other answer to my many questions was that it was 'fa'a Samoa'; setting it aside at once as something *sa* (sacred) and beyond the comprehension of the alien papalangi."

That was just the trouble, they thought over at Paramount, the picture might indeed be beyond the comprehension of the papalangi, or most of them.

Jesse L. Lasky, who had sponsored Flaherty, was strangely absent from the scene when *Moana* was unveiled to the public, leaving his colleagues the problem of selling it to the theaters. Four years had passed since *Nanook* appeared and gained a public for itself, against all prediction. Perhaps *Moana* would similarly disprove the professional prognosticators, but, on the whole, Paramount was inclined to doubt it. *Nanook's* drama had been as clear and strong as the contrasting blacks and whites of the old orthochromatic film on which it was made. The structure of this new film which Flaherty had brought back, instead of "another *Nanook*," was as delicate as the range of fine tones in its panchromatic photography, and the central dramatic device of manhood won by voluntary suffering seemed much too religious an idea for the motion-picture public as understood by those who successfully served it. Perhaps the Flahertys' self-doubts at Safune had been well-founded; perhaps fa'a Samoa was not a movie subject after all; certainly, the sharks and octopuses the Flahertys had originally gone after would have been far more palatable to the Paramount executives, even if they *didn't* exist. . . .

On the other hand, there were the ecstatic superlatives of the distinguished persons who had seen the film at its first preview performances. This was familiar ground. Paramount knew how to deal with superlatives and big names, but the company officials wondered whether these particular superlatives and luminaries carried much weight with the usual audience for Paramount pictures. They seemed addressed instead to another and far less dependable audience: specifically, to those numerous persons who continually denounce Hollywood for its failure to provide exceptional pictures but who, when the exceptional picture is by miracle provided, never quite manage to get around to seeing it, much less organize support for it. Flaherty insisted this public would respond if properly approached, and proved himself right, in his own eyes, by showing the picture successfully in six carefully chosen towns where, for once, the latent audience did turn out and support the film. Looking at the box-office returns from these towns, officialdom for a moment wavered. Perhaps this admittedly "special" picture ought to be road shown at high prices in the manner of a choice theatrical attraction, perhaps if it were given specialized publicity . . . But the doubting Thomases of the advertising and sales department prevailed in the end, and proved themselves right in *their* eyes by releasing the picture nationally in routine fashion. It was a turkey, a flop, a dog.

In the real or historical world, what this movie billingsgate means is that *Moana* earned a modest profit on its, for movies, very modest investment. But in an industry where profits of 300 per cent and more are possible, it's more fun to spend one million in the hope of making three than invest a tenth of that sum with the discouraging prospect of earning a profit of no more than one or two hundred thousand. Hollywood made up its mind. There was no money in Flaherty, great as his reputation might be. Better to file him away for future reference with that vast army of specialists, of one kind or another, who are called in when the "professionals" get into trouble. Flaherty was pigeonholed with the men you summon to help out with a difficult piece of camera trickwork or a snippet of ethnology. Till his death he remained there, in the mind of many a California brain-picker.

Well, there was always exploring. But the Flahertys, enthusiastic movie-makers now, to whom the movies were a closed door, couldn't bring themselves to give up. Hollywood was not all. The next few years were spent in making experimental films for museums and private sponsors; in conferring with Maude Adams, the energetic proponent of a Flaherty version of Kipling's *Kim,* in color; in a desperate, disheartening attempt to reveal the possibilities of the movies to foundations, benevolent institutions, and to a number of cultivated gentlemen from Wall Street who gave a connoisseur's appreciation to *Moana* but whose investment policies were identical with Paramount's. What Flaherty was trying to sell was, not only his own skill, but the immense audience he *knew* was waiting for the true film of the future. But though he spoke with the tongues of men and angels, the latent audience remained as immobile as a lump of clay. Again the thought occurred, as it had in Samoa, maybe nobody but us is interested in these things.

It happened, at that point, that a problem arose to darken the cloudless skies above the Metro-Goldwyn-Mayer studios in Culver City. M-G-M had bought the movie rights to the novel *White Shadows in the South Seas,* by none other than Frederick J. O'Brien, whose advice had sent Flaherty to Samoa. Irving Thalberg, troubled by the unorthodoxy of this "story property," perceived that it would have to be made on location. Association of ideas set in, and Flaherty was taken down from his pigeonhole, the man for the job, the round peg in the round hole. Still, there was the unimpressive box-office record of *Moana* to be considered. Perhaps it would be better to take out insurance. W. S. Van Dyke, considered an expert on "outdoor" pictures by virtue of his connection with numerous Westerns, was appointed co-director with

75

Flaherty, and, instead of the little family group which had gone to Samoa, a horde of first, second, and third cameramen set out for Tahiti. It was the behavior of the men from Hollywood, when they got to Tahiti, that revealed to Flaherty that he would never succeed in making a film out of his friend's book. Civilization was creeping into Tahiti, but it was still a terrestrial paradise. The tropic moon shone down on the beach, the soft waters lapped it, the Tahitians sang Polynesian songs in the coconut groves beyond, and, down on their knees in the sand beside a tiny radio, the cameramen were listening to Abe Lyman and his orchestra in the Coconut Grove in Hollywood. "Why not go back to California and make the picture in the Coconut Grove there?" asked Flaherty. He quit the job and sailed for home. Van Dyke finished *White Shadows*. Perhaps a dozen shots in the released version were by Flaherty.

Obviously, a man who would tear up a fat contract rather than turn drab facts into glamorized fiction was not to be trusted. But, one last time, his special abilities were sought by the commercial picture-makers. William Fox entrusted him with the making of a picture about the Indians of New Mexico. Production was stopped when first rushes revealed that the film was beginning to center around a small Indian boy instead of the "romantic leads" (white) whom Fox had sent along to adorn the tale. The film was never finished, and it was the last assignment Flaherty was to receive in Hollywood.

The Flahertys were preparing to take their children to Germany to go to school, when for the last time the South Seas beckoned. F. W. Murnau, celebrated director of the silent era, was leaving Hollywood in disgust. The same William Fox who had "trusted" Flaherty brought Murnau from Berlin to the United States, after the world success of his *The Last Laugh* and *Faust*. His first Fox film, *Sunrise,* was a memorable achievement, but succeeding assignments pleased him less and less and, at last, he parted company from Fox over a disagreement about the film *Our Daily Bread*. Murnau was a "studio director." He had learned his trade in the UFA studios at Neubabelsberg, Germany, which at that time led the world in craftsmanship. Their duplication of reality was uncanny, the wonder and envy of Hollywood. But to duplicate reality on the studio set you have to exclude reality. If the smallest bit of actual reality creeps in, the duplicate is revealed, by contrast, as no more than plaster and machinery. Nothing can be left to the chance observation, the unforeseen inspiration. Murnau was wholly the product of this kind of training, and his first American films were also "studio." *Our Daily Bread,* however, was laid in the Western wheatfields, which were important to the theme, and Murnau decided to take his cast on location to shoot "background," before getting down to work on the set.

Out on the prairies, something happened to this cunning artificer. Murnau became infatuated with the wheatfields as they were, rather than as they might be manufactured in the studio. He dropped his story and began to film the life of the land and the people, as accident put it in his way. Fox intervened; production was stopped, the film taken away from Murnau. It was finally finished on the Fox lot and released under the title of *City Girl*.

Immersed in his new preoccupation, Murnau sought the only film man he knew who had learned to wait on chance to provide him with natural drama. He proposed collaboration. Murnau's prestige would gain the pair financial backing; they would buy a yacht and sail round the world, filming as they went. That was all Flaherty needed; no sooner said than done. The bold pair set forth at once, turning contemptuous backs on Hollywood and all its works.

The first stop was Tahiti. "We'll make the kind of picture they wouldn't let me make of *White Shadows*," said Flaherty. This picture had, in Flaherty's mind, a specific theme, and it was not to be "another *Moana*." He did not want to record again the fading forms of fa'a Samoa, but the reasons why they were fading. It was a theme that had fascinated him for a long time — the impact of "civilization" on primitive cultures. Years before, in Baffinland, he had encountered Eskimos who had been visited by the whalers for centuries and who were as grasping and mean-spirited as the pristine Eskimos of Ungava had been generous, outgoing, and brave. It seemed to him that the first collision of two cultures resulted in the destruction of the moral fiber of both. The conquerors, unrestrained by the moral codes of their homeland, followed only their desires. The conquered, at first helpless prey, learned how to prey on others as soon as they abandoned belief in their old culture, which was anyhow being destroyed before their eyes. Both conquerors and conquered lived in an anarchic no man's land with no allegiances and nothing to believe in.

Behind the beautiful scenes of *Moana,* Flaherty had watched the beginnings of this; he had seen much more of it in Tahiti with the *White Shadows'* company. To Tahiti he now returned, to make a film that would show the West that its emissaries were not necessarily the torch-bearers of civilization, but, more likely, so many Typhoid Annies, bearing with them the germs of their own decay as well as the destruction of the people they sought to uplift.

Murnau-Flaherty Productions began operations in Tahiti in July 1929. The resulting film, *Tabu,* was released through Paramount early in 1931. It was reviewed as "one of the world's great art treasures." This may be, but it is a Murnau treasure, not a Flaherty one. The story, much of it, is Flaherty's; it was photographed under his supervision; and his name looms large in the screen credits. What is lacking is his signature in the film itself.

Murnau was an artist, by film standards a great artist and, in making *Our Daily Bread,* he had come to see that the motion picture derives its great powers from its own basic art of photography, rather than from the crafts borrowed from theater and literature. But, confronted with Flaherty's stark determination that the story must come out of Tahiti itself, and that the Tahitian story was that of the white man's exploitation of the native, his new-found vision failed. He wanted a more "dramatic" story; his civilized mentality called for civilized motivation, and he thought he had found it in a legendary version of the ancient Polynesian custom of the tabu. To Flaherty, the motivation as well as the plot that Murnau wanted seemed imposed on the people from without. The two men confronted each other. Flaherty's problem was worse than when he had walked out on a production rather than give in to Hollywood dictates. This was a case of two men of equal sincerity differing conclusively in their approach to the same material. Something had to give. Flaherty sold his interest in the film to Murnau and relinquished all control over its content.

Something of his original conception of the story can still be seen in the episode centered around pearl diving, and there is a memorable moment, drawn from life itself, in which a young Tahitian indicates his inability to take money seriously, much less to put upon it the value of life and death. But there was a more fundamental cleavage between the Murnau and the Flaherty approach than is indicated by story alone.

It shows in the photography, stamped all over with the style Murnau had developed in the old days at UFA. The stills from *Moana* and *Tabu* exemplify the difference better than it can be put into words. Flaherty's whole study was to give himself up to the beauty of the South Seas as they actually were. That beauty shines all through *Tabu*, but it is a beauty filtered and refracted through the imagination of a European of the twenties, who saw what he had come to see and had eyes for nothing else.

The two directors separated before the film was quite finished, Flaherty returning to the United States first. He was on his way to join his family in Berlin when, just before *Tabu* opened early in 1931, he learned that F. W. Murnau had been killed in a California automobile accident.

79

PART THREE
Aran

THE JOURNEY to Germany might well have been a journey
away from films, forever. Five years of trafficking with Hollywood
had resulted in nothing to which Flaherty would sign his name. It
seemed you were allowed to make films if you made them a certain
way, otherwise not. Maybe that was that.

It turned out differently. Something happened. Aboard the liner,
Flaherty fell into conversation with a young Irishman from Cork.

We got to talking on what was then the inevitable topic — the
depression, the hard times all over the world.

"Hard times?" he said. "You don't know what hard times are.
Let me tell you of the Aran Islands, where I have been. These
islands are barren rocks, without trees. Before the people can
grow their potatoes — almost the only food they can win from the
land — they have to *make* the soil to grow them in! For the rest
of their food they have to go to sea in little canvas boats, un-
believably primitive. And this sea they have to brave in these
cockleshells is one of the worst in the world."

I was thrilled. "Are these islands far away?" I asked.

"No," was the astonishing reply. "Just fifteen hours from
London!"

Soon after, I was in England. I hadn't been able to get the
Aran Islands out of my mind, and when I met Mr. Michael
Balcon, the brilliant producer for the Gaumont-British Company,
I found myself, almost unconsciously, telling him about Aran,
that I was sure a fine film could be made there — a film whose
theme would be the struggle of man against the sea. To my de-
light Mr. Balcon's response was enthusiastic and instantaneous.
Within a fortnight my wife and I made a survey of these islands,

which lie off the west coast of Ireland, thirty miles out from the old city of Galway.

The Aran Islands are three in number, and on the largest one, Inishmore, we decided to make our headquarters. The most important consideration was a supply of fresh water for our film developing, and Inishmore had a better supply than the other islands. Inishmore is nine miles long by about a mile-and-a-half wide, and has perhaps twelve hundred inhabitants.

Our crew at this time, besides my wife and myself, consisted of a young English lad, John Taylor, who could, and what is more had to, do everything. Later on our unit was joined by my brother David with his Akeley camera.

The first thing to do, and a most important one, was to choose from among the islanders some one to be the perfect diplomatist in our dealings with them. For when one came into a strange community to make a film of that community, negotiations to begin with were delicate indeed. This man we found in the person of Pat Mullen, who, though an Aran Islander by birth and preference, had traveled far in his earlier days and had spent seventeen years in America. Pat, a born leader, was just the man for delicate negotiations.

We established ourselves at a place called Kilmurvy, on the leeward side of the island. Here we were fortunate enough to rent from a London lady a fine cottage, the finest indeed on the island. There were two springs of fresh water nearby, and there was also an old stone wharf-house which might be made to do for our film laboratory. The cottage wasn't big enough for living quarters and a studio too; so, with island labor and the hard gray limestone rock of the island we built another — a real Irish cottage, with a turf roof covered over with a thatch of straw.

We were a good many weeks building the cottage and converting the old stone wharf-house into a laboratory. But all this time we were engaged in a still more important phase of our film production — that was, in gaining the confidence and friendship of the islanders, and more particularly looking for types suitable for the picture.

This is the method we have followed in all our films. We select a group of the most attractive and appealing characters we can

84

find, to represent a family, and through them tell our story. It is always a long and difficult process, this type-finding, for it is surprising how few faces stand the test of the camera.

One room was our "set," where we shot our interior scenes. This room was typical of all the cottages on the island, with a great open fireplace where in winter there was always a peatfire burning and a welcome for the islanders. Another room was our projecting theatre and cutting room, where day by day, and month after month the film was viewed and cut and gradually took shape on the screen. Our collaborator in the cutting was the able and enthusiastic young Englishman, John Goldman.

There are no motor cars on Aran, no movie theatres, no luxuries of any kind. The young man from Cork had not exaggerated the barrenness of the island. To the islanders their hard-won soil is more precious than gold. They would not part with a foot of their land, barren as it is, for any consideration.

Nor had my friend of the boat exaggerated the sea. All the way from America the North Atlantic sweeps in and hurls itself against the high rugged coast, sometimes climbing three hundred feet to the cliff tops and then sweeping in over the land.

Drowning here was no more than a natural death. Like most fishermen, the Aran Islanders do not swim. "The spirit of the sea is a monster, and must not be denied," they say.

All this was being shown to us and told to us by our dragoman, Pat Mullen. Pat wrote the story of what happened as we made our film in his book *Man of Aran*. He had never written anything before, so far as I know, but something about the filmmaking must have stirred up a creative fever in him, because ever since he set down this account of our Aran adventures he has been writing hard. He still lives on Aran, pretty much the life he always has lived, but his four novels have been read all over the English-speaking world and he has given something to the theatre too; his daughter is the lovely actress, Barbara Mullen. What follows is part of what he has to say about us as we made our film of the island people he was born among:

. . . While the work of building the cottage was bustling along, I spent some days driving Mr. and Mrs. Flaherty around.

85

They were interested in what I pointed out to them, but not nearly as much, so I thought, as other tourists that I had taken to these places before. But as I drove along the road Mr. Flaherty kept stopping me while Mrs. Flaherty took shots, as they called them, with a camera which she held up to her eye and clicked. We met and spoke to many people here and there along the road. Mr. Flaherty looked these people over very carefully with an eye to finding suitable people for his cast. We also visited people in their homes and chatted with them, partly to become on sociable terms with them and partly with the idea to find out if they would be suitable for the film. Both reasons were important.

One night there was a little bit of a dance in Killeany village. The Flahertys expressed a desire to go, so that they could get a chance to look the young people over. They did go, and there they saw little Michael Dillane. His appearance struck them so favorably that Mr. Flaherty was eager to get some shots of him. A few days later he did, but he had to take shots of Mikeleen's brother as well. The shots of Mikeleen came out very well, and though he took shots of many other boys, Mr. Flaherty never took any that he felt sure would fit as well as Mike's; so Mr. and Mrs. Flaherty then and there decided that Mike was the boy they wanted for the film. So they asked me to go to Killeany and speak to his parents about letting him come to Kilmurvy to go to work on the film. I did, and I painted Mikeleen's future in glowing colors.

"Well, now, Pat," said his father, "you know yourself that it is the woman who gets the most trouble from the children, so whatever she says herself I will be satisfied with it."

I had to see Mrs. Dillane about it many times. What questions she asked, questions which to me were absolutely senseless and time-worn, but which to her as to the majority of people of the Island were questions of more than life and death, because they involved the hereafter and eternity.

The Great Famine and its aftermath had left the Irish people frightfully poor and broken-spirited, and it was unfortunate that at this time some Protestant proselytizers attempted to change the faith of the poorest of them by setting up soup kitchens. In these places they endeavored to make the Irish people alter their faith in exchange for soup and a smattering of education! To this day amongst backward communities the fear of having their faith taken away from them by strangers, under the form of one line of endeavour or another, is a real fear.

Aran people were looking sideways at Mr. Flaherty and his talk of making a film; some of them believing at the back of their minds that his talk of a film was only a blind, and that once he had got a foothold and a grip on things the same old story would begin again but in a new way. Mrs. Dillane asked:

"What does Mr. Flaherty do, Pat, when no one is looking at him? Do you think he says his prayers? Some people say that he is a queer kind of a man. Do you think if I send Mikeleen over to him my son will lose his religion? Will they try to take it away from him?"

"Musha, don't you know, ma'am," said I, "that there is no fear of that happening? Those days are gone forever. These days everyone has enough to do making a living and they haven't time to care or think about what religion anybody else has. Besides," I added, "Mikeleen is a relation of mine through the Dillanes, and sure you know well enough I wouldn't be where anything like that would be tried on him."

She smiled faintly and said, "I believe that indeed, but if you want to know it, lots of people say that the divil a much religion you have yourself any more than Flaherty."

Rumours were rife that Mr. Flaherty was a Socialist. Not many on Aran know what Socialism means. To the great majority of them it means an organization backed by the devil. Other rumours had it that the cottage we had now nearly built was to be used as a "Birds' Nest." "Birds' Nests" were buildings or homes that were put up in Ireland during the famine years, and there destitute Catholic children were clothed and fed and brought up in the Protestant religion. So after all it was rather hard perhaps to place much blame on Mikeleen's mother. However, after some months we managed to get her consent. Mikeleen came to Kilmurvy, but for many weeks he did nothing but fool around the place, doing whatever he liked, except once in a while when I placed a little check on him. The rest of the cast had to be found before Mikeleen could be used.

Maggie Dirrane, the Woman of Aran, was glad to come and work for the pictures; it would mean a little extra money toward the support of her struggling family. Maggie has four young children, and though her life had always been a hard one, she always had a smile and a greeting for you, and the room would actually light up whenever Maggie entered.

Finding the Man of Aran was not so easy. And when at last we did find him, he didn't want to come at all. Colman King, known as the "Tiger," was a splendid specimen of manhood, a black-smith by trade, but also of necessity a farmer, a fisherman and a builder of boats.

By boats I mean the curragh, the frail fishing craft of the islands, survivor of the ancient coracle, a light wicker frame covered with tarred canvas — so light that on shore it has to be roped down so as not to be carried away by the wind; yet a better boat in a big sea I have never seen.

But to return to the Tiger — he was proud, dignified, and a bit aloof from his fellows. Several weeks of negotiating, however, ended in triumph. The Man of Aran capitulated and we were happy. Our movie family was now complete.

At night we had been having long talks about the sunfish or great basking shark, known in Irish as the Levawn Mor. Mr. Flaherty had never heard of these creatures before he came to Aran, but I could see he was excited by what I could tell him and I set about collecting all the information I could from the old men of the Island about this fish. In the old days these monsters were hunted by fishermen off the west coast of Ireland for their oil. Black hookers, boats of from about ten to twelve tons, were used, with five men to each crew. It was the one big moneymaking industry about a hundred years ago. My grandfather hunted them, and down in the old house tied on to a rafter over the fireplace I found two rusty harpoons. The flanges were encased in leather sheaths. In those old days the liver of the basking shark was worth as much as 35 to 50 pounds, it yielding up nearly 200 gallons of very fine oil, and was used principally for lighting purposes, in lighthouses as well as dwelling houses. The harpoons, including the flange, were from 4 to 4½ feet in length, the flange being about a foot long.

For years and years, for some unknown reason, these monsters practically disappeared from our coast, but about 6 years ago they came back in great numbers, and Mr. Flaherty decided that if the reports and stories that he had heard about them were true, he would throw back the film into the Aran days of long ago and take scenes of the hunting of the sunfish.

But who could tell us how to hunt them? "You will get no knowledge about the sunfish here, sir," one oldster said when I asked him, "unless you can get any from Martin Quinn. He ought to know something about them because he is up and down to a hundred years of age. But even if he does see you," he added, "I'm afraid he won't be able to give you much information, for I hear he is very slack. They say he is dying."

Though I hated to go into any man's house, bothering him, and he in such a weak condition, yet I badly wanted to find out how the great sunfish was harpooned, so I made up my mind to take a chance on going to Martin's house and maybe having a few words with him. I found the house and went in. An old woman was fixing jugs on a dresser. She was Mrs. Quinn, and after "May God save all here" and a few other remarks, I asked for Martin.

"You can't see him, sir. He is very sick. I am afraid he won't last long," said Mrs. Quinn.

I told her that I was sorry to trouble her, but I had come in for information about the sunfish, or as he would best know them, Levawn Mor, having been told that he was the only man now living in the Claddagh who could give me any information about them. If he could manage to speak at all, and if it didn't hurt him to do it, I would very much like to hear what he had to say about them. I also told Mrs. Quinn that I had known her daughter Mary in America and that she had often visited my house there, all of which was of course true. We talked about her daughter for a while, and then Mrs. Quinn took me into a clean little room, and in a nice clean bed I saw an old man covered up with the bedclothes, nothing of him to be seen but the top of his head which was covered with wisps of snow-white hair.

"Martin," said Mrs. Quinn, "this man has called to find out if you would be able to tell him anything about the sunfish, the Levawn Mor he tells me they used to be called. He is from Aran and he knew Mary well in America."

"Did he know Mary?" asked the old man as he feebly pushed the bedclothes away from his head. "How is she? And what do you want to know?"

"When I saw her last, the day I left America," said I, "she was very well; of course you know that she's married to Tom Brown. But," I added, "I want to know how you used to harpoon the great Levawn. We are going to hunt them again."

"Ha, the Levawn Mor," said Martin, " 'tis well I know them and 'tis them that's hard to kill," and his faded blue eyes shone brightly and took on a faraway look. Then he spoke again:

"You must have two hundred fathoms of line, with ten fathoms of it sarved near the harpoon end, so that when the Levawn rolls around on the bottom of the sea trying to get the harpoon out, the cable won't be cut on its skin. It is very rough and full of little sharp points and many a good boatman lost a Levawn that way long ago, for want of the cable being sarved properly."

"Where will I harpoon it?" I asked.

"On the grey streak under the big fin, but you are never sure of your Levawn till you drive home your second harpoon."

Then old Martin turned over on his other side with his face away from us, and as he pulled the bedclothes up around his head he again murmured, "The Levawn Mor."

It was not I, of course, who was to do the harpooning for the film, but Tiger King, but he, no more than the rest of us, knew anything about the way our people used to hunt the sunfish. Mr. Flaherty was in touch with an old-time whaling man, Captain Murray by name. They had met in the Northland when Mr. Flaherty was making a film called *Nanook*. Murray was then master of a ship working for the Hudson's Bay Company. They became great friends, and Mr. Flaherty had told us that if it were at all possible he would get Captain Murray to come over from Scotland, where his home is, in order to show us all he knew about harpooning. Word came from Murray that he was on his way to Aran, and soon after he arrived.

He brought with him a harpoon gun, and also some whale and walrus harpoons. The Tiger took possession of the gun, polished and cleaned it thoroughly. The Tiger had spent some time in the Free State Army, and he has a passion for guns. It was there he got the name "Tiger," because of his wild desire to charge the foe, it being impossible to keep him in an ambush.

March had come in with a breezy smiling face, and sentinels were now posted on the high cliffs watching out for sharks. In the meantime, Captain Murray had given us great help by show-ing us how to work our boat when harpooning — somewhat, but not altogether, similarly to the way he had worked his whaleboats when hunting the whale. We had been doing some thinking our-selves, but it took Captain Murray to show us where we should have a snubbing post put in and how to use it. Near the stern of our boat, against a cross beam, an oaken post was nailed and braced. Our line of one hundred fathoms ran from the harpoon back around the post and from there to the centre of the boat, where the main part of it was neatly and very carefully coiled. We also had another hundred fathom coil ready to be attached to the second harpoon. When the shark was struck we could all lay hold of the line from bow to stern of our boat, it being the best way to use our strength in order to get the most good out of it. Tiger was look-out man and harpooner, my part of the work at the snubbing post being to hold or slack away the line as the occasion called for, also to prevent the rope from getting snapped and to be ready to take a half-hitch on or off as the shark slowed down or sped on.

Mr. Flaherty had hired a steam drifter, the *Johnny Summers,* a fine, able boat; and from her deck, or rather from a platform erected on it, Mr. Flaherty took all the pictures of the basking shark for the film, and from our little pookawn we did the har-pooning. Many fish were harpooned from the *Summers* but most of them got away, as the boat was too heavy and didn't swing easily enough to the movements of the shark. With our pookawn, small and light in comparison, it was different. She swung easily. The

91

shark, when fighting, usually made a mad rush straight ahead, but by paying out a few fathoms of line gradually the boat was got gently in motion, so that the strain on line or harpoon was seldom too great.

The sharks were now becoming more plentiful, the weather had settled, and in high spirits we steamed through the North Sound with the pookawn in tow. Sharks were swimming round in great numbers. Mr. Flaherty was ready with his camera as we sailed amongst them. Captain Murray had the gun loaded with a harpoon sticking out of its barrel, but Mr. Flaherty said that we in our boat should do the harpooning. So we hauled our boat alongside the *Summers,* jumped in and cast off. We singled out one of the biggest sharks and rowed across the circle it made in feeding, in order to come nearly bow on to it when passing. This we believed to be the safest and best way to attack the fish, and this course we always followed except in breezy weather, when the sharks became restless and swam in all directions with the fin just showing above the surface. At such times we often had to row after them for long distances before being able to come close enough for a throw. In hoarse voices we spoke as we rowed, and gradually closed the distance between ourselves and the shark. Closer still — its snout was past our bows. Then, as if seeing us, it began to sink slowly deeper in the water.

Tiger stood in the bow, harpoon held high, waiting, and now the great fin was within reach, but going ever deeper.

The Tiger struck, and with a furious lashing of its tail that drenched us with water, the shark went down. The line ran out so swiftly that it smoked on the post and burned my hands as I tried to let it run clear. The Tiger had his axe in hand and a Barber knife between his teeth ready to cut away all, if the line fouled. The shark reached the bottom, and the rope slackened or became taut, and we had to haul in or give out according to the movements of the fish. Unfortunately after about half an hour clouds began to gather. Mr. Flaherty said we had better haul in and try to get the shark to the surface while the sun shone. We hauled away, and as we heaved we every once in a while looked over the side watching for air bubbles and movements of the water, which would give us an idea of how near the shark had come to the surface, so that we could be ready to drive in another harpoon.

We had taken in a considerable length of line when suddenly the shark tore away sideways from us. It had taken a couple of turns on the post. Hauling in an eight ton shark whose strength is not spent is no child's play, and we were badly in need of a few moments' rest, this being my reason for taking a couple of turns on the post. We were taken by surprise and, before I could get the hitches off, the boat had heeled over, almost gunwale under, and now the shark changed its course and was rushing past our stern.

The line slipped off the bollard in the bow, slid over and broke the thole pins along the boat's side, and now the boat was being towed astern at a furious rate. I had cleared the turns off the post to let the line run free, but now the shark went off at a slant downward, and whether our line was being dragged under a sunken ledge of rock or not I cannot say, but fathom after fathom of the line ran out. Still it went downward at a slanting angle. Tiger had flung his axe to me, and I picked it up and prepared to cut the line if the need arose.

"You have the end of the line," shouted the Tiger, "and the others get ready to cut away!"

The end had been tied to the thwart. Hoping against hope that even now the line would stop running out, I waited a few seconds longer, but now our boat was being pulled under. I raised the axe and was about to sever the line, when it parted — harpoon, line, and shark were gone.

We finished the day tired and somewhat discouraged. Mr. Flaherty worked his camera to the limit, but even so it was very hard to get much good work done. The *Summers* had to be bow or stern to the swell unless the day was flat calm, in order that good camera work should be done. Side on to the swell she rolled a bit, so that the camera often pointed to the sky instead of at the shark. On the other hand, the fish often swam in different directions, and many times it happened that when the *Summers* was in position, our boat was between it and the shark. In spite of everything, Mr. Flaherty was bit by bit getting material for his film.

On another day, about a mile from Hag's Head, we sighted a black fin low down in the water and cutting through it swiftly. Mr.

Flaherty suggested that I give the Tiger a hand on the harpoon. He wanted a shot of two men doing the harpooning. We manned our boat and rowed toward the shark. As we came closer I prepared for the quick run to the bow to help the Tiger, and then to jump back again to my place at the snubbing post.

It headed directly for us, swimming fast, and before we could swing our boat into what we now knew to be the right position, it swam right down by our side with its horrible mouth wide open, gleaming whitely in the green waters. Rows of small sharp teeth showed, and its wicked eyes seemed to be watching us, when with a final lifting of its snout over the water, for a last awe-inspiring look, it sank slowly down and disappeared from sight.

One of the *Summers'* crew shouted, asking us why we had not harpooned it, and I shouted back: "Oh, go to blazes!"

The reason we had not tried was because a shark swimming along from bow to stern could not be harpooned directly from the bow. The harpooner would have to move back at least as far as the shoulder of the boat, and then wait till the big fin was directly opposite him before he struck with his harpoon. While striking, a man must often lean far out over the side of the boat in order to reach the vital spot. Then comes the terrific thrashing of the giant tail and the harpooner is directly in line with it, as is for that matter every man on the boat. Our boat was lying low in the water. The tail of one of these sharks measures from six to eight feet across and a downward blow from it would either smash our boat to pieces, or, if coming with a fierce sweeping stroke from bow to stern, would crush us all to death.

I have read accounts here and there lately about these basking sharks, some of which say that they are harmless and inoffensive. This may be true, but I don't think that it mattered a great deal to us whether a shark meant it or not, when a sweep of its tail was able to smash our boat or knock us to Kingdom Come at a moment's notice! Boats ten tons bigger than ours had been lost with their crews that way in the old shark-hunting days.

On the other hand, rowing as we used to bow on, and a few feet ahead of the fin, the narrowest and strongest part of the boat was towards us, and as the great fish went ahead on its downward course the first furious blows from its tail struck the stem or strongest part of the boat; and when it came up over the bows the harpooner always had a chance to throw himself backward — and I believe now that it was due to this foresight on our part that we are all alive to tell the tale.

The shark soon appeared again some distance ahead, and we rowed hard to head it off. As it was crossing our bows, I unshipped my oar quickly and jumped to the Tiger's assistance. When passing Tommy O'Rourke I grabbed his cap and hair with my right hand and yanked it behind me, so that I could put on additional speed. Tommy's remark was unprintable! Tiger raised his harpoon, and as he thrust I threw my weight on the haft to drive it home.

With a furious thrashing of its tail the shark went down, and in that first plunge it very nearly took our boat under head first, a part of the line having fouled under a thwart.

Tiger raised his axe, but the line had cleared and the boat righted herself. This shark towed us about six miles, and we were continually hauling in or paying out line, as the rushing or the slowing up of the fish demanded.

At nightfall we got it alongside, drove in another harpoon, and after another hour's fighting we towed it into Kilmurvy, and the tide being low we anchored it. Next morning we rowed in to the shore with the fish lashed alongside.

Little Mikeleen and Maggie took part in the next scene of the film. Getting a huge boiler on props with the help of some men, they built a fire under it. They poured some water into the boiler in order to keep the liver of the shark from burning, the liver being treated in this way so as to get the oil from it. Then Maggie, when the oil was ready, poured some of it into a tankard, and she and Mikeleen took it home.

Sunshine, west winds, and low passing clouds favored this part of the story, and Mr. Flaherty's work on it is, I think, as beautiful as any ever shown on the screen.

All this time, little Mikeleen had been working on his part — that is, doing what most of the young boys used to do — fishing from the cliffs for rock fish, bream, and pollock. Fishing from a cliff 300 feet high requires a steady head and hand and also a great deal of experience, but Mikeleen, before he joined us, had fished off the Glassin rocks. His people have, as far as we know, always been landless, and have had to earn a living by fishing, so that at the age of 13 Mikeleen was already an old hand. He is surefooted as a goat, and is as much at home sitting on the edge of a 300 foot cliff as if he were in bed.

Mr. Flaherty had asked me if we should try to put a rope around Mikeleen and lead it back to a cleft in the rocks where it would be unseen by the camera's eye. Mikeleen would be safer that way. I didn't like the idea. Besides, Mikeleen had often told me that he wouldn't be able to work right unless he were free to hop around just as he always did. I also believed that had we put a rope around him it might have instilled in him a sense of fear, while being free would help to form his character — that is of course providing he didn't fall over! There was always the chance of his doing that.

On one of those fishing days, Mikeleen got ready his line, and we all went up towards Dun Aengus. Mr. Flaherty picked out with his camera the spot where Mikeleen was to fish from, and I must say that this same damn camera seemed to be possessed of the evil eye. It had the faculty of picking out the hardest and most dangerous places to get at. Mikeleen took up his position, and Mr. Flaherty shouting, "All ready!" Mikeleen swung his line around his head, letting it out in ever growing circles in order to get the proper drive to it. Then he let it go. It sailed far out because of the stone attached to the end; this is also used as a sinker for the line, and is attached to the line by a slender cord so that if the stone gets caught among the rocks the cord can then be broken by a sharp pull and the line saved. This sinker helps to place the line and bait in the chosen position, which is usually at the edge of or between sunken boulders, under which the fish hide.

Mikeleen jumped to the other end of his line, and lifted it high, letting it run out over his right arm to prevent it from being cut on the edge of the cliff, and also from burning his hands. When the line reached the bottom, he darted out to the edge of the cliff and sat down, his legs dangling over. He began to fish, feeling for a bit and balancing his line on the side of his pampootie to prevent it from being cut by the rocks underneath.

The place where he sat was split wide about 4 feet back from the edge, the crack being about 3 feet wide and 6 or 8 feet deep. The sea is forever gnawing underneath these cliffs, and in places they overhang fully a hundred feet, and are continually falling away into the depths below. Mikeleen was sitting on a large slab of rock that appeared to be about evenly balanced. One never knew when the cracked and broken cliff beneath would give way, but it had been like that for years, so we weren't much worried about it, and besides it seemed to be the very spot that suited the camera.

Mikeleen fished away, and after a time, believing his bait to be gone off the hook, he began to haul in his line. I shouted to him to hurry, because clouds were coming up and we wanted him if possible to catch a fish while the light of the sun was good.

When Mr. Flaherty had stopped using his camera, I jumped out onto the slab of rock to help Mikeleen pull in his line quickly. He looked up calmly from his perch and said:

"Pat, when you jump like that again, jump easy. The rock is stirring and it might fall out."

I was so shocked that I caught him by the collar of his jersey and dragged him and his line back to safety. I tested the ledge after that, and sure enough it was very shaky.

Mr. Flaherty sang out through a megaphone, enquiring what was the matter. I told him.

"My God!" he said. "If anything happened to that boy I'd never again touch a camera."

So, owing to the shaky rock, we had to look for another location. We found one inside Dun Aengus, and on these high cliffs Mike did most of his fishing. Not long after this, after a night's heavy rain, the broken rock where he had been sitting when it stirred, fell away, several tons of it.

We had to spend many days on the Dun Aengus location in order to get this part of the film as good as Mr. Flaherty expected the rest of it to be. It was tricky work because Mikeleen had to have a live fish so that it could be seen on the screen. He caught many, but most of them were either killed against the rocks on the way up the face of the cliff, or died "naturally." For rock fish as a rule do not live long when taken out of water. However, one day he hooked a real big fellow, and after great efforts and seemingly endless hauling, he landed it on top of the cliff. The day was fine, and luckily this fish, being very strong, stayed alive long enough for the camera to get a good picture of it. This completed Mikeleen's fishing scene, and needless to say we were all glad when it was over.

It was only a few days before this that Mikeleen called me aside and said: "Pat, I nearly fell over a while ago."

"I know that," said I, "but I didn't say anything when I saw that you weren't frightened, and," I added, "you remember I told you to be very careful because the wind was blowing strong from the north and against your back. I told you to brace yourself back against it in case it might blow you over."

"Oh, I knew that myself," said Mikeleen, "but what I didn't think of was my pampooties, and that the weather had been very dry for the past couple of days. The grass had dried and the rocks had too, and my pampooties were dry, hard and slippery, and I nearly fell out when I slipped."

It remained for us now only to get the big storm scenes that Mr. Flaherty wanted for the climax of the picture — scenes of the great windstorms that whip Aran every autumn and send the sea dashing right up and over the 300 foot cliffs. Everything looked favorable, for a strong gale blew from the west and a terrific sea was running. This was surely the day for us to get our final storm scene. It was important that we should, because Mr. Flaherty had got word that he must hurry to England with the *Man of Aran* film.

I had a long earnest talk with Big Patcheen and his men, and explained to them that this was the day of all days when the work must be done, because any day now this annual week of rough weather would be over, and no more storm scenes could then be taken, as Mr. Flaherty had to leave Aran soon.

They agreed with me, and said that they would do their best, but they went on to say that the day looked very threatening, and if the wind veered out to the south-west later on, which it looked like doing, we were sure to have showers of rain with squalls.

That I knew, of course, but looking Big Patcheen in the eye, I said: "We will finish the picture today, rain or shine, by hook or by crook."

We carried down the curragh and, while some other men held her, Patcheen and his crew jumped in, caught their oars and, after a final prayer and wish of "God strengthen your arms this day" from us on shore, Big Patcheen gave the word, the curragh was shoved off and they were away. These words from McDonough and Patcheen came back to me over the water: "Don't be afraid for us, Mullen."

It was now low tide, and the right time for our landing scene because the canoe had the best chance of running the breakers and coming ashore before the turn of the tide. At dead low tide the water is at its slackest; even the great waves seem to rest a bit before beginning their onslaught anew; at low tide the cove was somewhat sheltered and once a curragh was inside the breakers she was safe, but after the first half hour of flood tide it began to get dangerous, because Brannagh Island sound breaks across and into it in two places.

Amidst all this turmoil of water, the sharp-pointed rocks become exposed for an instant as a breaker rushes over them; then they are submerged again, and woe betide a curragh if one of those treacherous rocks grips her bottom; her whole framework is ripped to pieces as easily as one would tear a sheet of paper. Nor would there be much hope for the crew. The currents run so strongly that even a good swimmer would be helpless, assuredly being swept out to sea and dragged under. So that a landing is practically impossible unless done at the last hour of the ebb or the first hour of the flood tide.

"It will be an in and out day, Pat," said Mr. Flaherty, as heavy dark clouds were driven over the face of the sun. "We are lucky if we can do anything. I don't like it. That curragh out there is standing up against heavy weather enough as it is, yet we can't do anything without sunshine."

"The sun will be out again," said I hopefully, but to tell the truth I was becoming more and more uneasy. The clouds were banking heavily and, though the sun shone brightly in flashes, it wasn't staying out long enough for Mr. Flaherty to get his camera going.

Suddenly Mr. Flaherty would shout: "All ready, Pat. Will we signal her to come in?"

But before anything could be done the clouds had covered the sun again, and another spell of waiting took place.

I had the signal flag ready in my hand. When I raised it on high it meant that we were ready for the canoe to try for the passage, but it was understood between us that Big Patcheen was to use his own judgment absolutely in the running of the breakers. Time was passing and Mrs. Flaherty became very anxious.

"When is the turn of the tide, Pat?" she asked.

A heavy rain squall swept in from the sea and we had to seek shelter behind a huge boulder.

"The tide has turned long ago, ma'am," I answered, adding: "I know the men out there are in a bad position, but they are the pick of the best men, and with God's help the day may clear yet, so that Mr. Flaherty may finish his picture."

"Oh, Pat, I don't know," said she. "Not for the world, as I have told you many a time before, would we have anything happen to anyone engaged in working for us. At the same time, of course, you know more about those men and what they are able to do than I, so if you think the sun will come out and that there is not much danger as yet, then do as you think best. But just the same," she went on, "it looks simply awful out there to me."

Still Big Patcheen and his crew kept their curragh's bow to the sea, waiting and watching for the sun and the flag. At about half past one a rift appeared in the clouds, and we knew the sun would break through.

"All ready!" said Mr. Flaherty.

"A few seconds more," said I, "and we might as well venture it. You might get something done before the clouds come again."

As the last wisp of flying cloud was passing over the sun, I raised the flag, and the curragh headed for the passage; and being eager to get some good work done while the sun shone, they came on bravely. Glancing ahead, and on each side at the lines of breakers, Big Patcheen thought he would chance the run through. Half a dozen more strokes, eager though watchful as a hawk, he saw on the western reef a great sea rise up in a monstrous menacing black wall; a moment it towered, then it broke and raced towards them. Quick as a flash of light, six oars dipped as one. The curragh was turned out; a few strong stretching strokes and she was clear again.

The breaker tore across the passage with a roar as if of rage at being cheated of its prey. The curragh went farther out on the deep.

"Was there danger then, Pat?" asked Mrs. Flaherty.

"Plenty of it," I answered. "Any other men in that boat would never get through."

She looked at me with one of those strange looks she sometimes gave me, as if trying to find out whether I had not become quite heartless and cared not a jot whether men lost their lives or whether they didn't, provided the film was finished. I do admit that at this time I did have very strange thoughts, and like Mrs. Flaherty I too have sometimes wondered. But indeed the making of *Man of Aran* was enough to make any man think strangely.

"All ready after the shower," I shouted. "The sun will be out when the rain passes."

The curraghmen were also watching. The rain passed, and as the last shadow sailed past the sun I hoisted my flag. The curragh came in closer, but now the great seas broke clean across the passage, the rush through could not be made, and the blue patch of sky was being pushed away hurriedly by heavy black clouds. It seemed to be an entirely hopeless situation, and yet if those breakers just lowered for only a few minutes, Big Patcheen might make a try for it.

"Ready! Ready!" I shouted, as I saw the oars snap forward. On the reef the breakers still reared high, but not so high it seemed as they did a few seconds before. Yes, they were trying, those great picked men of the west. On they came through those mighty seas, rowing strongly, yet finding it difficult to make much headway because of the terrific undertow. They disappeared down into the trough of the sea. My heart stood still, and through our minds on the shore the same thoughts flashed: will she ever be

101

seen again, will she win through? Yes, we see her again, and the superb skill shown in her handling by Big Patcheen and his men bring wild cries of admiration from Shauneen Tom and some other men who had by this time gathered on the shore.

A great wall of water lifted its length on the reef. It was the first of three great breakers. Higher it rose as it gathered its strength for destruction, and from the men on shore the cry arose: "Ah God! Give them strength, it is coming! It is down on top of them. They are lost!"

But they weren't lost. The curragh had come through the worst of the passage and now as this monster sea came raging toward them there was a chance to fight it, and this Patcheen and his men, with superhuman effort, prepared to do. I shall never forget the thrill it gave me, when I saw Big Patcheen with a left-hand stroke, his men timing their strokes instinctively with his, get ready to meet the crest of the wave, and how McDonough flashed up his right-hand oar to let the cap of the sea go by.

It was not a question with us on shore now as to whether the sun shone or not. To have the curragh land as quickly as possible was the first thought in our minds. Mike and Maggie were on the shore; I had pointed out to them the place where the curragh must land — that is if it ever landed — and all through the curragh's battling with the waves they shouted and signalled to the crew pointing to the only spot where as a last chance a curragh might make a run for it.

Mrs. Flaherty hurried to where I stood, and looking at me beseechingly, said, "Oh, Pat, Pat, can they ever land?"

"I will tell you something, Mrs. Flaherty," I answered. "They cannot land, that is come ashore in any way that a curragh ever landed before, as far as I know. The day has turned out so terribly bad that they cannot go back out again through the passage, and I'm afraid after another hour and a half the curragh will be lost in the channel, because the high tide will come breaching over that ledge of rock. That is the only protection they now have from the whole force of the western ocean."

As the curragh topped a gigantic wave, and then disappeared out of sight, Mrs. Flaherty cried out: "Oh, my God!" She turned away and covered her eyes with her hands. "What shall we ever do if anything happens to those brave men?"

"I wouldn't take on as bad as that," I said, "because there is still hope. Patcheen believes he will never be drowned, and when a man believes that and knows his business besides, 'tis hard to lose him!" I told her some more about how I had impressed on his mind the dire necessity of doing the work this day, and what it meant to Aran and to the Flaherty family.

She looked at me very reproachfully and said: "May God forgive you."

Now and again a spot of blue appeared, but Mr. Flaherty was working his camera in sunshine and in cloud, all the time shouting: "Can they make it, Pat? Can they make it?"

Such work as these peerless curraghmen were doing could never be done again. Time and time again they tried to make a landing when the great seas were not coming through all three channels at once, but they were driven out again and again to continue fighting what now seemed to be a losing battle.

Shauneen Tom turned on me, his face white and his eyes blazing, saying: "Oh, you ruffian! You have the men lost! There is no blame coming to the Flahertys, but *you* know what kind of a sea ran here with a high tide and a storm."

"You are right, Shauneen," I answered, "but even so, I have hopes yet that Patcheen will make one big try and he will either live or die in the doing of it."

"I know," said Shauneen wildly, "that they are three as good men as ever caught an oar. But there is no curragh that was ever laid on sea can last there much longer."

The curragh was now being tossed and buffeted here and there by the force of the seas. Patcheen and his men trying fiercely to hold her in a favorable position so that if the chance came they might be able to run for the shore. Three times we could see they almost fancied their chance had come, but with lightning strokes they had driven their curragh out again. Great monster seas tore through the Brannagh Sound channels. This last time, that they rowed out, there came in front of them a giant wave, bellowing in through the south passage, and, though we on shore had thought

103

that it was from the seas in the Brannagh Sound channels that Big Patcheen had expected the danger to come, we soon saw that this was not so, for by far and away the biggest sea of all that had come up to this time came rushing in through the south passage. This was where the real danger lay. It might have caught and driven the curragh against the Brannagh Sound breakers, and, had such a thing happened, nothing could have saved either men or curragh.

We didn't know that when Patcheen saw this giant wave coming that at last he had sensed his opportunity, and he prepared to take advantage of it. He rowed out to meet this wave before it broke. The curragh topped its crest and disappeared from sight down the other side. The great sea broke, and came raging into and through the channel and on to meet the other breakers racing in from Brannagh Sound.

We looked and could hardly believe our eyes, for the curragh had turned in after it had let the great wave pass, and now here they were rowing with all their power for the shore, putting into their work the last atom of their strength. Patcheen had taken the slender and only chance of the giant wave being able to overpower and hold in check the seas from Brannagh Sound long enough to enable him to reach the shore. It was a long chance but it was the only one, and he was taking it. Would they come through: They should now be able to hear our shouts of encouragement, but our shouting suddenly turned to cries of dismay, because farther in and directly in front of them, sometimes clear of the foaming water, sometimes hidden in it, were those treacherous rocks.

"Run her in, Patcheen! Run her in!" was shouted from the shore; but it was almost impossible to drive the canoe against the current, and before Patcheen could head the curragh for the straight short run to the shore, another sea came roaring in from the South Channel, and he had to swing his curragh's bows to meet it. The current dragged her relentlessly toward where death lay lurking. As the curragh swung around, those rocky fangs came up dripping white and seemed to reach out for her, but death missed Patcheen and his crew by a foot; with superhuman strength and uncanny skill they had managed to hold the curragh about a foot from the cruel toothed rock as she met the next sea bows on, while the next breakers came foaming in; she was turned in again

104

Aran

"All the way from America, the North Atlantic sweeps in
and hurls itself against the high rugged coast"

THE LEVAWN MOR

"What shall we ever do if anything happens to these brave men?"

in the flash of an eye, and was now running straight for the shore.

Shauneen Tom and some others were for rushing down, but I cursed them back, for here was a chance to finish the film, as Mr. Flaherty had planned, and I now depended on Big Patcheen and his men being able to save themselves without any assistance from us.

As the canoe was driven up on the rocks, Patcheen and his men leaped out of her. A great sea was rushing in, and after one glance at it, to judge its power, they ran up over the rocks to safety. The oncoming sea caught the curragh, dragged it out and smashed it to pieces, and this last sea finished the *Man of Aran*.

Patcheen and his men were drenched with sweat and brine, but their blue eyes were lit up with blue fire, and a great thrill of wild pride shot through me as I looked at them, for here had been a trial of some of the old, old stock, and the blood still ran true.

Shortly after this, Mr. Flaherty took the film to London and after a few months he sent me word to have the shark-boat crew, with Mikeleen, Maggie, and Big Patcheen, all in readiness to sail for London in order to add some dialogue to the film.

I didn't have such an easy time with Maggie, because rumours were flying around that we were going to a pagan country, consequently she was a bit shaky about going. However, she finally consented.

After a little over a week we got ready to go to work at the Gainsborough Studios. We found it terribly stuffy after the free breezes of the Isles. We didn't have much bother in putting the dialogue in because we all remembered, more or less, what we said when working on the different scenes in Aran. But of course nearly all my cursing had to be left out, which seems a pity because most of it was very brilliant and flowery! Mr. Flaherty took Tiger, Maggie, Mikeleen and myself to the British Broadcasting Corporation building where, as was usual with us now, we were treated very kindly. We broadcasted a little bit from there, and then we were taken to see the latest thing in television, which was truly wonderful. The Tiger, however, was not impressed; he said that he had visioned television fifteen years ago!

A few nights later was the big opening of the film at the New Gallery Theatre. I went there with very mixed feelings. Here, at last, after about two years of effort, made up of joyful moments when some good work had been done, and of days, weeks, and months of disappointments when it seemed impossible ever to get anything to go right, here at last was the final test. We were all there in film costume. My father was with us, and to look at him one would imagine that it was he who had made the *Man of Aran* film instead of Robert J. Flaherty.

The theatre was packed full with well-dressed men and lovely women, beautifully gowned. The picture was put on the screen; it was run through, and then, as we of Aran stood up in our seats, the house rang with applause. Handclapping and cheering filled the air. My father, though a little man, felt big as a giant. Maggie was very pleased and had a wonderful expression of happiness on her face. Mikeleen was very proud, but the Tiger maintained his stoic expression, and Patch Ruadh said simply in Irish:

"They seem to be making a lot of us; they are giving us a lot of praise and credit for working on the picture and helping to make it what it is; all of them seem to be happy." Then he turned to me and said earnestly: "And, Pat, God knows tonight that I'm glad they are happy."

A lot of pictures were taken of us as we left the theatre, and here and there one could hear remarks passed: "The men of Aran — yes, that's Maggie." "That's Tiger," and so on.

We were a bit shy and got away as quickly as we could. I was very happy that night, because we had been through a lot of heart-breaking work in the making of the film, and it was a joy to know that our work had not been in vain.

We stayed also in Dublin for a week, and we were present at the opening night of the film at the Grafton Theatre. Here too it was a big success and I was much thrilled when I heard some women say during the great storm scene: "Oh God, bring them safe in."

Mikeleen, Tiger, and Maggie got a wonderful reception as they appeared in the doorway after the show. Mikeleen and Tiger returned to England to travel around the cities there in the interests of the film. Maggie, Patch Ruadh, my father and I returned home to Aran, to live again the lives we lived before we went to work on the film.

PART FOUR

India

M AN OF ARAN, an international prize-winner, captured
more attention and praise than any other Flaherty film since
Nanook. It was a press sensation. But its box-office record paral-
leled that of all its predecessors. In London, Paris, Rome, Berlin,
and in metropolitan America, where its maker was personally
present to see that it reached audiences which would like it, it
played to packed houses. Elsewhere, where it had to depend on
ordinary movie distribution and exploitation methods, it was lost
among the B films. This mixed reception was not financially impressive enough to rehabilitate Flaherty as a good risk in the eyes
of most movie gamblers. But there was one magnate whom it did
impress, because he was on the lookout as much for prestige as for
money.

The international success of Alexander Korda's *The Private
Life of Henry VIII* had established Korda as the savior of British
films. Backed by City millions, he now looked beyond Britain toward the world film market. The handsome studios which he built
at Denham were intended to be an international movie Mecca, a
rose-garden colony to which the gifted of all the earth would re-
pair, and out of which were to come films which had to be great
because so many admirable people from so many countries were
connected with them. Among the flashing names that decorated
the Korda diadem were, already, Charles Laughton, Douglas
Fairbanks, Sr. and Jr., and Elisabeth Bergner; soon to join them
were Marlene Dietrich, Josef von Sternberg, Sir Laurence Olivier
and H. G. Wells, while even Winston Churchill, then in the politi-

109

cal wilderness, wrote some scripts and Sir Robert Vansittart some lyrics. And here was Robert Flaherty, his *Man of Aran* laurels fresh on his brow. True, he had never been able to fit his talents into the commercial scheme of things but, in a way, that very fact made him precious to a seeker of glory. He too must pull a jeweled oar in the Korda galley. Frances Flaherty has described the circumstances cordially enough:

Wherever we took our camera, from one primitive scene to another, we used the native people as our characters and took our material from the stuff of their lives. We found what good actors native children can be, and how appealing they unfailingly are to an audience. So we had this idea; why, if we wrote a film-story around extraordinary adventures that a native boy might have in his native environment, wouldn't it be possible to "star" that boy himself in the film?

We set about to write a story that might film. This was not very congenial practice for us. We usually worked from the barest of outlines, preferring to "find" the story in our material. However, experience had also taught us that to gain backing for a picture, something had to be offered besides my husband's enthusiasm for places and peoples — something on paper.

The first story we wrote was of a Spanish boy, and it was based on an actual happening — the pardoning by public acclaim of a famous Spanish fighting bull in the bull ring. Our story, following the adventures of the two together, developed the devotion of the boy for the bull up to his pride and agony in the final life-or-death scene. It was a good story. But we were uncertain whether we could show a bull on the screen and make him so convincing in his lovability as to be sufficiently appealing and sympathetic. With what animal, we asked ourselves, would it be easier to do this? Why, of course, with that great lumbering, antediluvian pet, the greatest oddity and most peculiarly engaging of all God's creatures on earth — the elephant! Our story shifted instantly to India. What more intriguing than the adventures of a little Indian boy on a big Indian elephant in the jungles of India with all the jungle creatures?

But who could be found to produce such a film — a film that depended on a "star" who was a mere boy, and a native boy at that, a quite ideal boy, moreover, who had yet to be discovered by some one of us somewhere in India! This needed a producer of no little courage and enterprise. Fortunately there was such a one in London. There was Alexander Korda. Almost before we realized it we found ourselves on his production schedule under the working title of "Elephant Boy."

But, Mr. Korda now remembered, there was already a famous story of a boy and an elephant that almost everybody knew — Kipling's *Jungle Book* story of "Toomai of the Elephants." Immediately the necessary arrangements were made between Mr. Korda and Mr. Kipling and the film rights to the character of "Little Toomai" and of "Kala Nag" and to the Kipling title were ours. And the rights to the Kipling story as well, if we wished to use it. The Kipling story revolves about an elephant dance — the "dance" of wild elephants in the jungle at night. This was pure fantasy. Or was it somewhat fact? Was anyone suggesting that we should find — or make-believe — an elephant dance in the jungles of India for our film?

Anyway, our minds were full of other pressing and more practical questions. Where in all India would we go to make the film? To British India or to a native state? Where, first of all, were the wild elephants? Most of them were way off in Assam, in remote jungles. But there were plenty too in the jungles of Mysore in south India, hardly 800 miles south of Bombay. Would His Highness, the Maharajah of Mysore, an exclusive and conservative ruler, be graciously disposed to let us work in his domain? Would he let us have his elephants? For we needed a quantity of tame elephants as well as wild ones.

With all these questions still in the air, my husband, Bob, his brother and assistant, David Flaherty, and my daughter Barbara set out for Bombay. By the time, six weeks later, that I was ready to follow them, all had been settled — settled by the permission of H. H. the Maharajah of Mysore, and on the warm recommendation of the Viceroy, Lord Willingdon, who said that he couldn't think of a better place for us to go.

111

The two younger Flaherty daughters, Monica and Frances, stayed at school in England during most of the film-making, and as a result, most of this part of the Flaherty story is recorded in letters which their mother wrote them from India. It was a happy chance that things fell out so, since, as John Collier wrote at the time, "These letters are not works of art, but works of nature. Nature has certain advantages — naturalness, among others. And for authenticity there is nothing to beat it, as those artists admit who marry their models. By good luck, which again belongs to nature, these casual letters tell a story, or at least follow its contour. The story is that of a Flaherty film. A Flaherty film differs from others; the making of it is an adventure rather than a gamble. It is an exploration into a sort of beauty that cannot be put 'under contract.' "

The letters originally appeared in Mrs. Flaherty's book *Elephant Dance*. To aid them in "following the contour" of the story of *Elephant Boy*, I have here combined as well as condensed them. This is Mrs. Flaherty's own introduction of them:

"Lest there be any bothersome confusion about them, the members of the Flaherty family who will be met with in these letters are: my husband, 'Bob' or 'Daddy' — Robert Flaherty, producer of films; his brother and assistant, David Flaherty — 'Uncle David'; our eldest daughter, Barbara, 'Barbie,' with us in India; and the two younger daughters, Frances and Monica, at school in England most of the time, though they did come to India while we were there. These last are the 'Darlings' who were chiefly responsible for this spilling of ink."

May 28th, 1935

DARLINGS:

We have found our house. Daddy calls the film a "natural," the way everything is breaking for us — the ease with which we found the house. A house with great elephant heads carved on the entrance gate; a young palace, all for the asking, ideally situated on the outskirts of the town with free vistas of open country, spreading shade-trees full of monkeys, cheetahs prowling at night, derelict walls, and "quarters" probably full of snakes. Moreover, it is on an old, blood-drenched battleground where Tipu Sultan, the most lurid usurper of the Mysore throne, fought the English. They say the cries, tramp and tumult of battle still sound at dead of night. Here we will live during most of our film-making.

Daddy and I went to see it today. It was all shut up when we got there, with a guard in uniform, a soldier, very formal and rather suspicious of us, in charge. Daddy wouldn't take a step inside until all the doors and shutters were wide open. 'Fraid of snakes. I must say it hasn't the air of inviting anybody in. It's a bit forbidding; massive, square, high-ceilinged tile and plaster, about as human as a stone statue and as mysterious. It was built for the Maharajah's grandmother ninety years ago. A fortune teller in Paris once told me I should be "equally at home in a hut or a palace." I suppose this is the palace. Daddy says we must have snake-charmers come in and clear the place of snakes before we settle in.

June 28th, 1935

Things are beginning to happen thick and fast. First of all, cobras. The yard is full of them. The first one was caught just at our doorstep. Last night the watchman found another. The two caught were young ones, so evidently there's a family of them. The bite of the young ones is as deadly as that of the old ones. A cobra in a bus in Madras bit first the driver, then three passengers one after another, and all four died, so potent is cobra venom. I can tell you we watch our step! No one has lived in this palace of ours for so long that the creatures have been undisturbed for years.

This morning there was a shout of "Cobra!" from the yard, but it turned out to be only a tree snake, a thin, speedy, vivid green thread of a thing, with an arrow-pointed head. Again there was a shout from the "quarters" side and there was a whopping big scorpion caught in the shed. Great menagerie we have!

113

July 4th, 1935

This morning early the yard was full of strange pipings, and looking out of the window I saw five figures spreading out over the dirt plain behind us, where derelict ant hills, riddled with holes, denote the abode of the cobras. So far no good. They have piped and played in vain. We wait for the noonday sun to add its potency to the charm. Meanwhile, out of an innocent-looking basket are pulled half a dozen captive cobras to dance for us, their wicked hoods outspread. They dance and then with a "swush" they give a wicked lunge and strike, are picked up by the tail or anywhere, and gladly of themselves slide back under the dark cover of the basket again.

The charmers say the snakes are hibernating during the monsoon, far, far underground, so far they can't hear the pipings. So they probably won't come out any more, anyway, until it gets hot again.

On top of this the big palace elephant, Irawatha, came towering in through our elephant gates to pay us a visit. He is the biggest elephant in Mysore (nine feet eight inches). I had a ride, clambered up over his tail-end and sat on a pad, hanging for dear life on to the pad ropes. It was nice on top; easy gait. We went out on to the road and collected some huge branches for fodder and came marching in again. I haven't had such a thrill since I was "so high." I do love the old beasts. They are too wonderful. I gave Irawatha a loaf of bread, about as big as a crumb to him, and he rumbled in his throat to say "thank you."

I don't think I told you we have a tribe of monkeys here, perfect pests; lots of fun. Can't leave windows open at night or they are all through the house, and anyway their funny faces are always peering in at the windows, squatting, hopping on the sills, finally all retreating to the big trees out back, where they attend to their own affairs with swinging and shrieking.

We caught a baby monkey. I confess we wanted it with a view, of course, to film shots. We nursed it in our spare room; fed it off the fat of the land. It ate, but it cried and cried, pitifully, screwing up its little mouth with such a world of melancholy in its pathetic little eyes. And the unhappy mother hovered about, peering in at the baby through the window, moaning. When all the other

114

monkeys had left, she still stayed in the yard, jumping from tree to tree.

At last I couldn't stand it any longer. I took the baby onto the roof. The minute the monkeys saw it, what a bedlam of shrieking and chatter broke out! I thought I should be mobbed. The mother came leaping to the nearest tree. The baby saw her and began to shriek and struggle in my arms. I slipped the leash. One leap and it was at the edge of the roof, one more and it was in the tree, one more and, oh, my soul, in its terrible fright and trembling hurry it had jumped short.

I saw it hurtling through the branches, and closed my eyes. I heard it strike the ground. I was a murderer, no better. No, thank goodness, the little thing was up and running for dear life, straight into the wide open door of our new laboratory. I called out. The whole staff turned to, and the laboratory was searched. A few minutes later out came Ranga Rao, holding at arm's length a small thing dripping wet. The luckless little creature had jumped straight into a tub of water. Yes, it got back to its mother. No more baby catching for us. I thought the monkeys would hate us and desert the compound. But they didn't. Next day they were all back, swinging and shrieking in the trees again; even the baby.

But the other day in the road a monkey was dead. None of our men would touch it. Instead they went to fetch a priest and rose water and incense, in order to perform a proper ceremony to bury it. Yes, the monkey is sacred.

The laboratory I mentioned we have fixed up in the old servants' quarters of the palace — an ideal place for it.

It is about the only thing here that is like old times. You know how Daddy likes to travel light on his expeditions, with as little extra work, as few people and as little outfit as possible. It is easier that way, less distracting. There are not so many people and things to keep going then, if one might wish to stop, once in a while, to think. But this Indian film is different. There is to be no stint of people and everything possible to help us make the picture and make it quickly; which is all very good fun for our large Indian staff; for our confreres from London as well, who are enjoying the whole thing with us.

I wish you could see us here! How you would open your eyes!

115

It is so different from the way we did things in Samoa and Aran that we hardly know what to do about it — so many people about, doing for us all the things we have usually had to do ourselves — a fleet of cars flying here and there, a lorry as full of people as a Sunday School picnic plying daily from town (two miles) to our "bungalow"; thousands of cameras; thousands of racks, bursting, bristling with tripods; a stills department with two assistants and I don't know how many still cameras; thousands of carpenters, electricians, tailors, bearers, coolies, sweepers, mahouts, animal trainers, clerks, accountants, interpreters — you would think we were a bloody factory!

July 20th, 1935

We went for a drive this afternoon. Now we are in the midst of it, India does seem populous, a continuing human stream, and Daddy swears there are more cattle than people. The bullocks and buffalo are beautiful and so are the carts. And the goats (for goats) are especially lovely. As for the slender women, in the upward curving line of their saris, balancing lovely things on their heads with delicate arm, elbow, wrist and finger upraised in a lovely bow, they are beautiful — especially when they are carrying two brass pots one above the other, like a golden temple decoration. Then with their shining pots they group themselves around a well, these women! Oh, there wasn't a sight along that whole road that wouldn't have made a picture and used up rolls and rolls of film.

The Mysore bullocks are not as patient and long-suffering as they look. Like elephants they obey only their keepers, and are dangerous to all others; also like elephants they have a long memory and will bear a grudge. Several keepers tried to make their bullocks lie down for us, pulling on the rope which passes through their tender nostrils, but the obstinate beasts wouldn't.

Late in the afternoon is the time when everything begins to happen along the road, and I love to be out in it. There is the never-ending wonder of the sheer numbers of the droves and droves of cattle, and the goats as delicate as deer, with pointed horns and delicate hoofs that patter along the road like rain. They pour out from the jungle where they have been grazing all day.

The herd girls and boys, mere children, stare out of big eyes and tousled heads. They dare the jungles and the jungle roads, I suppose, because there are so many of them. The same with the slow procession of bullock-carts, never-ending day and night.

From end to end of India they trek unceasing. It is like a sort of nightmare to think of it. It is like the migration of ants one sees, no beginning, no end, unbroken, crowding, jostling, a whole mysterious way of life beyond all common comprehension. As they go creaking by, or stop, resting with their bullocks in the shade, I must always scan the faces of this vast company of the road. Some are wild and fanatical, some gentle and fine. The faces of women and children peer out from the frames of the oval basket-work hoods of the carts. I wonder at the great size and iron weight of the teak logs they carry and what else there is of cargo to keep them ever moving, moving.

Yesterday we took a long drive to see one of the monumental sights of Mysore, a colossal Jain statue. We went on until we came to a hill that rested on the plain like a huge boulder. We had to be carried up it, swung on the shoulders of four bearers in a sort of wooden cradle. I did pity the poor bearers puffing and sweating in the full heat of the hot afternoon. They put down the cradle every now and then and mopped their brows and smiled at me.

As we approached the top of the hill, we saw the great stone head and shoulders against the sky. It is an immense statue, the biggest stone figure in the world carved out of a single block of granite. Wrought with utmost simplicity, there is yet such a feeling of the texture of flesh about it that you wonder it can be stone. Its date is A.D. 883, and yet it is as fresh and perfect as though it had come yesterday from the sculptor's hand. The figure represents a seer who has stood so long in the perfect immobility of profoundest meditation that the ant hills have grown up about his feet and the vines entwined his limbs. Once every while there rises up about the statue a huge scaffolding. This is for a ceremony — one of the ceremonies of India's cult of fertility. Votaries swarm in every part of the structure and pour milk, human milk and sacred cow's milk, over the figure. The face is unforgettable. I shall always think of it, looking out over the wide plain.

Everywhere there are great statues because everywhere there are palaces — four thousand years of them — and temples, temples of all the faiths India has known, some of them still worshipped in, some abandoned in the jungle. Barbara and I photograph them forever: statues, sculptures, friezes, a whole lost life in stone. We can only guess at the stories they tell, for no one really knows any more, but sometimes we meet somebody who can tell us the legends about them.

August 3, 1945

We've got a little elephant boy David picked up somewhere over in Malabar. He is an endearing kid. He is bright as a dollar: learning something every minute; learning to repeat his part. He isn't a real mahout boy, but he isn't a bit afraid. He climbed right up on a big elephant when even the mahout's son didn't want to.

We have three other boys besides, that we have gathered from here and there all over the country to try out for Toomai. I watch them playing around, kicking a football, shouting and fighting like kids everywhere, and think of the strange stroke of fate that is hanging over one of them.

There is one boy among them whom Bordie (Mr. Borradaile, our chief cameraman) brought in the other day; found him at the elephant stables. He is different from the other sprightly little sprouts. He is rather pathetic, more reserved, an orphan. His mother's family came from Assam, where the people are part Mongolian. His name is Sabu.

August 5, 1935

Yesterday we were invited to Karapur to take part in an elephant shoot. We have practically decided on Karapur preserve as the best location for our jungle scenes and it is time to reconnoiter, since we will be shooting them as soon as the monsoon is over. I dreaded the shooting part of this expedition but we have to have experience and get acquainted with our jungle and wild actors, and with the jungle men.

Little Sabu went with us, the little mahout boy we picked up at the Maharajah's elephant stables. He has been gradually eclipsing the three other boys for the part of Toomai. He was so thrilled

118

to be the one chosen, while the other three clung about the car, crestfallen.

On the way to Karapur, we came upon the hunting elephants we had met a few days ago, having a glorious bathe. They were coming out of the water all clean and black and shining. I loved seeing them again, like old friends. I could imagine they recognized us. We made much of them, patting them. The one I thought so old is not old at all, not full grown, but she had a bad time, poor thing, bearing a calf which was born dead. Her eyes are so patient and kind. Though only a year and eight months caught, she seems gentlest and wisest of all.

At Karapur, Sabu was in his element, thoroughly at home, ordering the elephants about, mounting them, riding them, sitting there as on a throne from which he looked down upon us common mortals. It was here, by the way, near Kakankote, that he was born. His mother died when he was a baby. His father taught his elephant to rock the baby's cradle — to rock the baby himself in his trunk. It is even said that a wild elephant came out of the forest and played with the child!

The river was mightily swollen by the heavy monsoon rains — a racing torrent three hundred yards across. Daddy was curious to know if the elephants would tackle such a current and asked the mahouts if they would care to try it, offering a most attractive reward. They were all willing but in spite of their most violent urging, not an elephant would go beyond his depth and face the stream.

Finally the chief mahout came down, and we asked him if among all his elephants there was one strong enough to swim the river. Yes, he had one. It was Lakshmi Prassad, a big tusker.

Lakshmi forthwith was made ready for the swim. A rope was put around him, by which the mahout would be enabled to hold on against the raging current. Sabu, very busy, kneeling on Lakshmi's broad back, helped strap the rope around him. The mahout mounted to his seat on Lakshmi's neck. Sabu settled himself, sitting behind the mahout. He was going too! I didn't like it. I was afraid. Was it surely all right?

They launched into the river. The bank was sheer and almost at once the elephant had lost his footing and was swimming, swimming strongly, his head up, and then under, up and under. Midstream the current caught them, a swirling, whirl-pocked flood. The elephant could make no more headway and began sliding downstream. He was now completely under, only the tip of his trunk showing, and Sabu and the mahout were down to their armpits. We were in a panic. We had not guessed the river's strength. Twice, Sabu told us afterwards, he lost hold of the rope. Just as well we didn't know that as we watched him — his little figure holding on for dear life, the mahout, and the head of the elephant bobbing like a cork as the current bore them down, down.

Below them, fortunately, the river made a wide bend. Here at last they touched bottom and clambered up on shore. We all broke out shouting. Sabu waved. There was no longer any doubt who was to be our elephant boy!

August 25, 1935

When we came back to the bungalow this afternoon, Irawatha, the elephant who is to play Kala Nag, was having his lesson. He and Sabu were rehearsing Scene One. Everyone was laughing delightedly to see them. The big elephant was stealing the sugar cane out of Sabu's hand, raising his foot to be punished and squeaking, all to order. Sabu, his little brown body in nothing but a tight-fitting breech cloth, was a perfect thing of beauty.

I sometimes have an uncanny feeling about Sabu. This is the boy we *imagined* way back in '29 when we were writing our story. We wrote down in so many words:

"He is a little orphan boy and hanger-on of the Maharajah's stables."

And then we wrote:

"His father died, and the elephant, the beloved elephant who had been in the family since his grandfather's time, went mad with grief and broke his chains and went off into the jungle."

And now here is Sabu in the flesh, a little orphan boy, ward of His Highness's stables. And they have been telling us the story, how when his father died his elephant grieved so that no one could do anything with him and there was nothing to do but take him to the jungle where he ran away — our imagined story and

120

Sabu's true story almost identical. It was as we were writing our story that all this happened to Sabu, six years ago.

September 28, 1935

Something happened last week that made our hearts almost stop. I have not recovered from it yet. This is what Daddy wrote Mr. Korda about it:

DEAR MR. KORDA:

Since cabling you last Sunday we have been shooting continuously, with perfect weather and good results. The monsoon has at last passed away, and I expect no hold-up from weather from now on.

Mr. Biro [the late Lajos Biro, chief scenarist for Korda] ever since we first started the story, has been nursing a pet scene which I was rather reluctant to undertake. The scene in question is one in which, while Little Toomai is proceeding through a crowded street on his elephant, the elephant inadvertently walks over a baby. We tackled the scene last week. Having secured the mother's consent, we placed the baby in the street, and called on Sabu and his elephant. There were hundreds of people about, all intensely curious. We started our cameras. Irawatha, looking like a walking mountain, approached. The tip of his trunk went down and momentarily sniffed the baby. Then on he came. Each of his ponderous feet were thicker than the baby was long. Slowly he lifted them over, the baby looking up at him, too young to understand, of course. Then the elephant's hind feet came on. The first one he lifted over slowly and carefully; but the second foot came down on the baby's ankles. I never heard such a yell in my life as that which came up from the hundreds of staring native onlookers. Someone swept up the baby, while our camera crew made a circle around it to keep the crowd back, jammed it with its mother into a motor car and raced off to the hospital. I thought there would be a riot, but fortunately nothing happened; and before we had the cameras struck, the car came racing back from the hospital. The baby was smiling and the mother was smiling. When we ran the picture that night we could see that the elephant, as soon as he

121

had felt the touch of the child's feet, had thrown all his weight on the outer rim of his foot.

He is truly a marvelous elephant. He picks up our Sabu by his ankle, holds him up in the air, and walks around with him. He picks him up in his trunk and does what we were repeatedly told would be impossible, lands him up on his head, on his back, or wherever the boy tells him to.

(Please don't mention this incident of the baby to the press. I have already been accused of trying to drown a boatload of wild Irishmen on Aran!)

Everyone is happy here. There has been no sickness of any moment, and I believe that every last man is in high spirits over the film. Mrs. Flaherty and myself and all the staff send all good wishes.

> Sincerely yours,
> ROBERT FLAHERTY

September 1, 1935

Yesterday, a white spot appeared on Irawatha's temple between his eye and his ear where there is a little hole in his head. From this hole, fluid oozes out when an elephant goes "musth." "Musth" is a sickness male elephants have, during which they go mad. They always recover, but the sickness is severe while it lasts. Today we learned that Irawatha is indeed "musth," which means that we cannot work with him until he is well again, and nobody knows how long that will be — three weeks or three months.

He stands doubly chained by his forefeet and hind feet in a place by himself, and no one is allowed to come near him. He looks terrible, and his eyes are wild with pain. He cannot keep still. His head is never still but nodding and nodding and swaying and swaying, up and down and from side to side, and every once in a while he lifts his trunk up, and lets out a heart-rending cry. Daddy got out the cameras and filmed him. He had the mahout throw him a bunch of leaves as though urging him to eat, and Irawatha, his head still swaying, swished it up in his trunk and swished it around and finally threw it in a completely mad gesture over his head, where it hung awry, like Ophelia's wreath. The poor elephant was most evidently in the depths of an agony that made you feel very sorry for him.

September 3, 1935

Bob always has the luck. I told you that our elephant, Irawatha, went "musth." It was an ill wind that blew us plenty of good, for in the pictures we took of the poor creature in his painful, uneasy state, he looks just as we want him to look in the story when he is "grieving for his master"!

The film begins to look like something. The casting is over and the first third of the picture, all the opening scenes, are shot. And now for our big dramatic scenes in the jungles we are taking a fresh leap into the unknown and incalculable.

September 10, 1935

We are coming to the part of our Indian experience that we have been waiting for, dreaming of since we dreamed of India at all, as all people do — of that strange, exotic, perhaps terrible, always exciting place they think of as the Indian jungle. All the rest of our film will be shot in the jungle.

We have moved to our jungle location, Karapur. Our camp spreads out from our own bungalow in rows of white tents. Everything was brought from the palace in Mysore — bearers, cooks, cars, trucks — a bare skeleton was left behind — and we have settled down here in Karapur.

One wants to sit by the river all day long and watch the river village people come and go; a strip of shining beach, bamboo behind, river before, and these beautiful people out of a fable with their slender, fine cattle, shining pots, flowing saris and inimitable grace and graciousness. They are just getting water and washing themselves. But what a thing to see!

It was not until today, when we ventured into the jungle, that I began to realize I really was in elephant country. I watched for the milestones to change to black. All the milestones, elsewhere shining white, in elephant country are painted black, because elephants hate white and will root the white stones up.

On the way back we saw the elephants that are kept for the

teak work. They were having their evening bath and scrub in the river, throwing water over themselves and rolling in the water on their sides and grunting and rumbling with content. There were eleven of them, several good big tuskers and one big cow, with a dear kind eye, who was only one year out of the jungle, but so gentle that we could pat her trunk, and I loved her on the spot. I can't get over either the strangeness or the complete loveableness of these creatures. Their mahouts are a people apart.

November 6, 1935

Last evening we watched the "night training" of a twenty year old tusker caught that day and highly bid for at auction that afternoon. He was superb, short but thick gleaming tusks, tremendously powerful shoulders and head, and his eyes — how can I describe it to you? I have seen wild elephants at later stages of their training, but in this one I saw an elephant facing the fires, the smell, and the cunning of humans for the first time.

He was tied between two trees — stretched hind and forefeet between them. Slowly a group of men approached with burning torches. The elephant recoiled, because there is nothing that terrifies him more than fire. He swung his head from side to side, his eyes dilated and blood-shot, straining at the ropes; but the men approached nearer until they were surrounding him. Then they started chanting, and while one man waved a torch up to his eyes, the others gently rubbed his sides and legs with sticks. At first he was terrified, then bewildered. The chanting, the continuous motion of the rubbing, and the fire swinging before his eyes seemed to act like a drug. After an hour or so he began to sway drunkenly on his feet, righted himself, swayed again and tottered. As soon as he was about to collapse the men stopped their chanting abruptly, raised a shout and prodded him with their long spears to startle him into a standing position again, only to repeat the whole operation. It wore the elephant out as nothing else could — until, after a few hours, they left him to rest.

The training as it goes on by day is more kind. The mahouts praise the sufferer. As he is marched up and down and up and down between them they chant to him; they praise his fine long tusks; they tell him of the big jemadar who caught him, of the rich man who will buy him, of the golden howdah he will wear one day, and of the weddings and processions and fairs he will see — and fair women . . .

There are elephants that are born and reared in captivity, but these, I am told, never make the "good" elephants who work and obey and become the devoted life companions of their keepers that these wild ones do. For the essence of the relationship between the man and the animal is that the wild spirit has been broken — like a broken thing this strange, great heart in the queer great body clings for life to the only thing that is now left to it, its only security, this human who has taken it and made it his own.

November 8, 1935

These forests have been the scene of many famous elephant drives or "keddahs," superbly organized. All through the forest are forest huts and forest rangers experienced and seasoned to the work. Four miles from Karapur is Mastagudy, an elephant camp, with twenty work elephants. Four miles beyond that in the forest are the ditches, post holes and rotting timbers of elephant stockades, still standing from the days of the old keddahs.

Just how we finally came to the decision I don't know. It seems to have grown out of the circumstances. A magnificent wild herd such as has hardly been seen before; the old keddah sites, so easy to reconstruct, all there; the forestry organization just ready to be set into motion; and, above all, the certainty of getting our pictures in this way as in no other — all these things conspired together. We decided to have a keddah, a real keddah in the traditional style; to call all the villagers from miles around to make a small army (1100 actually) of beaters, to pair these with jungle men, and to call out the forest officers to captain this army: to build the stockade and runways — an engineering feat of timber (10,000 pieces) and rope (9 tons); of digging and chopping and hauling — with hundreds of carts and all the work-elephants engaged. It sounded like a tremendous undertaking for just a film. A keddah is staged in Mysore only after many months of preparation and only for one most important occasion — the visit to Mysore of a new viceroy or of royalty.

125

November 11, 1935

We have surrounded the big herd. On the banks of the river we have put up machans for our cameras. And the first thing we are going to do is drive the herd past them into the river and across it. There we will again surround them and hold them until we are ready to drive them again, this time back across the river, into the stockade. The stockade is being made ready. Beyond the runway wings extend along the river bank. The two gates at the entrances of the stockade and runway are gigantic things, specially constructed to swing up like a trap, and crash down by cutting a rope.

The herd is hemmed in by fire lines, built by the beaters. No wild elephant has been known to face fire. The only animal, Bob says, that isn't afraid of fire is the bull moose. He will charge it, even charge the headlights of a locomotive.

November 12, 1935

Today, all day long, we have not left the cameras — hoping for the herd to come to the river to drink and bathe and play. Our cameras are mounted on platforms, camouflaged, on the foreshore of the river. Lined along the high bank behind us were the beaters beside their fires, to keep the herd from crossing. Should they start to cross in our direction we were to film as long as possible and then run as fast as possible for the bank and up it until out of reach. It was too steep for the elephants to climb. It looked too steep for *anyone* to climb. I picked out a spot with plenty of tree roots sticking out for a hand hold.

Probably we hardly realize what a sight it is to see those elephants. Muthanna realized it. There are forest rangers who live their whole lives in the forest, he says, and are lucky ever to see an elephant at all. No one here ever saw such a sight before. The herd come to the river because there is no water in the surround. If there were only full grown elephants they would come at night. But there are a lot of babies and it is better for them to bathe while the sun is still up.

Six o'clock. The sun was almost setting. Sh . . . Muthanna with his fingers to his lips. After our whole day of waiting here they were coming at last.

126

I opened my big lens out to the last stop (2.3). A big tusker stood on the bank half hidden by the bushes and all we could see was his trunk raised above them, this way and that, feeling the air. I was sure he would get our scent. The wind had died down. It had been favorable to us all day. Now there were currents going every which way. Yes, he had turned up the bank. The game was up. He had smelled us.

But no. Half way up the bank he paused and then . . . The jungle screen along the river became alive, and drifting out of it and down the bank came the herd, more and more, until we counted more than fifty.

I was glad my lens was so fast. Still the light was terribly flat. The young elephants and babies sported in the water, their black heads bobbed up and down on the surface. The bank was steep and they climbed up on their knees and slid down on their haunches (by this time it was too dark to shoot any more so I just watched them), while three enormous cows stood guard on the bank, watching the children and throwing dust over themselves.

The big tusker came wading along up the river and told them it was time to get back. A younger tusker remained behind, long after the herd had disappeared — though his little sweetheart waited for him just at the jungle edge — and though we dismounted our camera and packed up and made no bones about noise, he was still there, keeping watch, when we left.

We made our way through the jungle back to camp in the falling night. How hard to believe that there was anything in that soft, sweet jungle beyond, sweet with the smoke of sandalwood. For there is nothing sinister about the jungle, not so much so as in those dark, witch-like forests of Germany. It is all sweet and kind. Among the trees, so tremendously tall, stretching upward, we might have been in a cathedral. I cannot understand these fierce hunters with their tales of ferocious experience. As Bob said, he felt like a murderer watching that charming domestic scene of the wild elephant families at the river side, thinking what a bad time we are going to give them, when all they ask is to be let alone in their paradise. The elephant has no living thing to fear but man. Probably that is why so often one comes upon other game near an elephant herd — bison and sambur. They are there for protection.

127

As we came back to cross the river, a thin, milky mist was over it, making it look ghostly in the moonlight. The half moon mirrored in black pools between the rushes, and picked out in shining circles the slow swirl of sluggish currents. Like watchful, crouching eyes, the red gold fires of our beaters along the bank were doubled in the water.

Saturday, January 4th

Today was the Day of the Big Drive. Operations started at 6 A.M. As we came down the road, two hours later, the morning mist was still in the air like fine rain. From the elephant camp, the seven tame cows picked for the drive were just starting off to cross the river, where the beaters were waiting their coming to begin the day's manoeuvres. First the eastern wing was to be moved up over half the area, the beaters carrying firewood with them to establish a new line. This done, the tame elephants would move up to the apex of the two lines, and the final drive, straight through to the river, would begin.

From 2 P.M. our orders were to be in our machans, absolute silence, no smoking. Overnight our machans and the stockade had been camouflaged; elephants had been tethered all about to destroy the scent of man. Elephant neither see well nor hear well. (How much more careful we had to be with the crocodiles. You just knew that across the whole width of the river they could see and were watching every move.) The elephant depends on his trunk, scenting the air.

Our big lenses were pointed, like machine guns, at the shore, raking it up and down, not to miss the first rush breaking over. Then bang, bang! There they came. But only for a moment, half a moment. They turned down stream *out of sight, out of sight,* they crossed the river below us, and before we could even change our lenses, before we could think, there they came pounding along directly under our machan, a bellowing, lurching sea of rushing backs, pouring into the stockade. A complete rout, alas, for our cameras. Behind them came the yelling beaters, brandishing their torches.

Saturday, January 4th, 1936

The drive is over and eighty elephants, as near as we can count,

"Daddy calls the film a 'natural' "

"From end to end of India they trek unceasing"

"There was no longer any doubt who was to be our elephant boy!"

Irawatha, "Musth"

Flaherty's elephants, India

The studio's elephants, London

are in the stockade. And two enormous tuskers. The most spec-
tacular herd ever driven, a triumph for Muthanna. But what a
pitiful sight to see them, their panic just like the panic of a crowd
of people, all regardless of each other in their one idea of safety
for themselves at the centre of the milling circle, butting, pushing,
jabbing each other, and making terrible noises, groaning and sob-
bing like the tortures of hell. Many of them show buckshot
wounds. The big tusker has a raw hole behind his eye; a big
cow's eye is blind with blood. There are several babies, one tiny
one; probably the baby to whose birth we were almost witness
when we visited the herd where they stayed in cover so long. The
big tusker is the one that gave me such a thrill when they bathed
in the river. Another tusker, almost as big, they say, is one that
has been caught before; there are old rope marks on his legs.
He is a "bad one," therefore.

They are putting on a wretched show now. Every once in a
while a maddened mother, with a high piercing trumpet, will
charge the stockade. But not the tuskers; they are not at all brave
and use all their tusks and weight to hold the centre place and
jab the lesser ones away. I am so afraid the babies will get crushed.
A half-grown tusker was down in the mud on his side. By this time
the whole stockade was a slimy, slippery mass of black mud like a
stye, and smelling to heaven just like a stye.

Sunday morning

A baby goes down in the slippery mud of the stockade, under
those huge milling bodies. It will be trampled. The Jemadar won't
allow it; goes into the stockade, ropes the baby and pulls it to the
barrier and they get it through. The little fellow isn't hurt, full of
beans, and oh, how thirsty. It can't drink with its trunk, too young,
but there's water on the ground and water in a shallow dish, and
its silly little trunk wobbles and splashes and tries to find its mouth.
"Oh, how I'd like a good drink!"

We catch its trunk up and open its mouth and nearly choke the
little creature pouring water down its throat. But still with its
funny little trunk pressed down in wrinkles into the mud, it tries
to get the rim of the bowl in its mouth. It is too funny. The brown
faces watching are a study. They do love the little thing. They

start leading him, protesting, to the river. At the river brink: "No, I won't go in. I won't go in without mother. Mother said not to go in without her." But once in, oh boy, what a long, happy drink. "Now I've had enough. Let's go back to mother." The poor mother, as it passed the stockade, had followed it around.

Tuesday, January 7th

It is all over. The elephants are gone back to their lovely jungle, the beloved beasts.

I hated to come down to the stockade to face hearing again their unceasing moaning and groaning from the depths of their agony and torture. It seemed to me the sounds were worse, more despairing. The sudden screams seemed like the last extreme of endurance. They were human cries. They were like the boar in Samoa whose dying agony has rung in my ears all these years. It was unbearable. We all broke down. Three o'clock was set for the opening of the gates to let them go, set them free. Such a relief; I had to turn away into the bushes to hide that I was crying.

The baby is o. k. At first I thought he was dead, stretched out on his side, asleep. But it was just as sweet and peppy as ever, the center of an admiring, loving crowd, bringing it milk and water. But what to do with it? The herd, even the mother, now that it smelled of humans, would not take it back, would probably kill it. It might be raised by hand, it might be fostered by our tame mother cow elephant, sent up to her to the palace stables. A woman came and poured water over it from her shining brass pot. The baby wallowed delightedly in a puddle of water and mud.

Throwing bundles of straw and rice into the stockade and watching eager trunks reach out was some consolation. They crowded to the barriers to pick them up, even the big tusker became a hungry baby.

Everyone was having a guess at what the elephants would do — once the gate was open — whether they would come in a rush or come slowly, whether they would stop at the water and drink, whether they would take the deep water crossing straight ahead or shepherd the babies to the shallows at one side.

And there was our baby, being brought down and let loose

right under our machan. Perhaps, we thought, the herd in its excitement would take it along, perhaps the mother would find it. The little thing instinctively wandered up to the enclosure and along the stockade to find Mother where he could hear her voice, I suppose, among the others. If it stands there by the stockade gate, I thought, it's the end. He'll surely be crushed by the first out-rush.

The tension during the final clearance of the runway under our machans I can hardly describe. A fifteen minute call before the gate was open. Are you ready? Yes. I was on a low machan. I was warned to draw my dangling feet up for fear the big cow might spot me and try to mount our tree. She had tried to climb the stockade; she had learned to reach up with her trunk to the stockade machans. Our machan was firmly built into the branches of the tree. I was glad of that. Most of them hang dizzily out from the bare trunk, slung from iron stays fixed to the tree by spikes.

The elephants came out in three sections, rushing, not stopping at the water edge, right out into the deep crossing. While snapping frantically, I watched anxiously for the baby. He wasn't with the first section. There was a tiny one with the second section, but no, it wasn't ours. I watched it, wee thing, bravely swimming, its little head a black, bobbing dot in the water getting further and further left behind by the big ones. Oh baby, baby! But just then, as though at last the dam had burst, the final section, the main herd with the big bulls, came tumbling out with a roar, an avalanche of bodies, big and little, in a rolling cloud of dust.

Last of all the enormous tusker, tail up and prodigious stride, as though hell were after him, and at his heels, our baby, running and running with all its little might, so tiny. "Oh, big Daddy, here I am. I'm coming. Don't forget me." They struck the water, and as they struck it their trumpeting became a tremendous roar. Daddy said it was wonderful to hear in the microphone. They struck out to swim. Baby, oh baby, striking out after them, so terribly little. By the time he had struggled to midstream, the herd was over.

And for agonized minutes we watched the little thing struggling, dazed, going round and round in circles, expecting every instant to see it go under. "Save the baby!" I shrieked. I was crying. Then

131

a raft came gliding toward the wee head, the little creature was seized by the ear, and half on the raft, half in the water, held up by a rope round its body, it was towed across to the far shore. A great shout went up and waving of torches from our side. The baby, exhausted, lay in a snug nest of sand and slept. Two watchers stayed by it. Early in the evening the mother came down and took the baby away. And so ended our keddah.

Mysore City,
March

We have been writing our story, re-writing it. For three weeks we have done nothing else. It has been a hard task — has torn our combined brains to tatters and drained them white — such an effort — really terrific. But we are pleased with the result. The mould is finally cast; now to give it life.

If we do it well, the film will have something in it of this quality of legend and deep natural mystery. You see, the great natural spectacle in our story was to be a wild elephant drive into a keddah stockade — regular whoopee.

Our drive came off splendidly, our captured herd was a magnificent one. We let them go again and took pictures of them coming and going. When we saw our "rushes" a miracle appeared on the screen — no semblance of a drive, but instead these most extraordinary creatures, as if in the heart of their mysterious jungle, "going places." Where were they going? Why, to the Elephant Dance, of course, just as it is in Kipling's story. So we re-wove our story all round this elephant dance. All we need to complete the illusion is their feet in action. All our camp of twenty-five tame elephants has gone into training like a ballet chorus — to learn to dance. Isn't it a quaint life?

So now that our script is beyond the peradventure of further change, we can go ahead with our work as fast as possible. Our Kala Nag, Irawatha, has gone "musth" again. But still we talk of going back in May.

The whole Indian adventure has been a fairy story. There is magic in the very air, and the beauty of it acts like a drug — a timeless dream. No one has painted or sung it adequately because it seems to be inexpressible.

Postscript, London, Feb'y 14th, 1937

So many people ask me what has happened to Sabu. As I write
he is here in London. He is very happy. Every time I see him I
ask him, "Aren't you homesick, Sabu? Aren't you tired of London?" But he answers with always the same smile on his lips, the
same light in his eyes. People stop him in the streets and ask, "Is
this the Elephant Boy?" They know him from his pictures in the
papers.

We brought him to London because there was still work for
him to do on the picture in the studio. There was dialogue. And for
six weeks through the whole night, in the penetrating cold misty
nights on the banks of the Colne, he worked in nothing but his
loin-cloth, evidently suffering no cold. Not a sniffle has he had all
this winter in London.

The studio went wild about him. His acting amazed them; they
called him a genius. They insured his life for fifty thousand pounds
and set their best writer to work writing for him the story for
another film.

But in the meantime our own picture through months of work
in the studio has been steadily mounting and mounting — soar-
ing — into the realm of "big" productions. And Sabu must carry
it all.

That *Elephant Boy* had soared into the realm of "big" productions was not the doing of the Flahertys. In the two years since
Korda had sent them to India, things had been happening to the
rose-garden colony at Denham. The big names had come, bearing
their prestige with them, and departed with their prestige and a
considerable amount of cash. And returns from the dreamed-of
world market were frighteningly slow. So, when the *Elephant Boy*
unit arrived in London with its footage and its young star, de-
cisions had to be made.

Prestige alone, it seemed, could not bring in enough money to
pay the rose-garden overhead. And here, suddenly, was the prime
prestige picture of them all, a Flaherty film lightly based on Kipling but drawing its real inspiration from the land and people of

133

India as the Flahertys had seen them. Well enough, but it would after all be necessary to pay some attention to tried and proven box-office formulas. Following Kipling, Flaherty had made Kala Nag go mad at the death of his master. This might be well enough in a book, but for movie audiences some more Occidental motivation might have to be supplied. Why not a wicked keeper, whose cruel treatment of Kala Nag causes his madness? That was it! And if a keeper, then his cruelty would have to be acted out at the studios in Denham — explained by means of dialogue in a whole new series of scenes. It was clear that Flaherty's original aim of filling the sound track with the life of the jungle, with only snatches and fragments of dialogue supporting the essentially visual story, as he had done in *Man of Aran,* would have to go by the board. This new story-line required dialogue and plenty of it, and, since there weren't many Hindus around London, the parts of the mahouts and beaters and bearers of the elephant jungle would have to be played by white movie actors with Oxford accents. . . .

With this studio filming the Flahertys had little to do, and for the first and last time they allowed the editing of their material — the giving to a picture its definitive form — to go out of their hands into those of "professionals" more accustomed to telling stories along familiar lines than to trying to render the unfamiliar, the unknown. The resulting mixture can be judged through a comparison of the studio-made scenes with the pictures which precede.

It wasn't altogether the disaster such a comparison might suggest. James Shelley Hamilton gave a sympathetic view of it in the *National Board of Review Magazine:*

> For the first time Robert Flaherty has put himself within the restrictions of a story-book plot in this film. Usually he goes to life itself and lets the simple relations between man and nature be his story. The results have been annals of primitive family life against a background of earth, sea and the elements, far removed from ordinary movie drama, virile and lyrical and lovely.

Something of natural beauty as well as something of the thing called "documentary" had to be sacrificed in this Kipling tale about the boy who followed the old elephant out into the jungle at night and saw the fabulous elephant dance. The story had to be expanded. This plot business is all to the good for those who need plots to be interested in, and doesn't get particularly in the way for those who find their fascination in the elephants, the boy Toomai, the glimpses of India and the jungle. Some of the minor characters may seem to have come from a casting office, with beards stuck on with gum instead of being nature's growth, but they do their bit toward keeping the story moving and obtrude very little in the splendid panorama which in retrospect seems to be so much vaster than some of its details would appear able to add up to. For Flaherty has accomplished his customary magic and recreated one of those far-off places the ordinary person can only read and dream about, and put it vividly and beautifully.

PART FIVE

The Land

Elephant Boy was the last film which Flaherty was to make for any branch of the commercial motion picture industry. Hollywood showed no further interest in taking him down from his specialist pigeonhole and Flaherty himself, after those studio scenes at Denham, had been wary of making the sort of compromise which they represented and which alone would restore him to favor. It seemed possible, as the depressed thirties wore on, that he might never get the chance to make another movie. He may have thought this himself, for he devoted his energies in those years to other forms of story telling — in books, magazines, and on the BBC.

But in the time since *Nanook* the form he had invented had been developed by other hands. In England, an excited group of young journalists, sociologists and educators had organized what became known throughout the world as "the British documentary film movement," which aspired to use the Flaherty method of filming primitive peoples to dramatize the problems of industrial civilization. In the U.S., the New Deal gave Pare Lorentz the opportunity to follow a similar tack with *The Plow That Broke the Plains* and *The River,* and the success of these memorable American documentaries whirlpooled Lorentz into the headship of the United States Film Service, an agency set up by Presidential directive to provide "government reports on film" about the administration's program. Lorentz invited Flaherty to return from England to make the first of these.

The picture was to be made for Henry Wallace's Department of Agriculture and the theme was to be that cluster of interrelated problems stemming from soil erosion and including sharecropping and migratory labor. And 1939 seemed just the moment for such a film. America was reading *The Grapes of Wrath,* and people were shocked at the discovery that millions of Americans, men and women like themselves, had somehow got shut out of American life, left to fend for themselves against actual starvation. Too, Wallace's ever-normal granary plan was just then a topic of white-hot controversy. The auspices seemed favorable for Flaherty's first attempt to use his own medium in the manner of his disciples — to make a "problem" documentary.

Some sort of script had been prepared for him in Washington, but as usual the Flahertys discarded it and took to the road, traveling their own country for the first time, filming as they went. They went South to the cotton fields, West to the irrigated, mechanized farms of Arizona, North through the dust-storm states to Iowa and Minnesota. They "covered" the American agricultural story as no reporter had covered it, on film or in print, but they returned to Washington with a sense of insecurity. As Flaherty had written to Jay Leyda, early in 1940, ". . . The truth is that I am sweating pretty hard over the film I am trying to finish for the Government. I never tackled a tougher or more confusing job and there are times when I don't know whether I am standing on my head or not."

Their coverage was vast but diffuse, and to them it lacked focus. Their general theme of the waste of the land took them to so many parts of a big country that they were unable to settle down and live with any part of it; they had had to catch what they could on the fly, and move on. In doing so, they were departing from the essentials of their own method and it troubled them. More than any of their filming, the footage they brought back with them represented a sketch of their intentions rather than the hard-won but unblinkable finality of their earlier films.

What they faced when they got back was worse. While they were gone, America had begun to mobilize for defense and to help Britain's lone-hand war against Hitler. Every government policy of the early New Deal days had been altered, agriculture's most of all. Officially, the land problem was no longer that of conservation but of getting marginal lands back into cultivation as quickly as possible. The human problem was not one of unemployment but of where to get farm labor to replace the young farmers who were going into the armed forces. Even while Flaherty was making his film, its theme had dated irrevocably.

All through the hot summer of 1941, Flaherty sat in Washington with the Department officials, struggling to make sense of a picture which was at war with events. What finally emerged was a divided film. Its dramatization of the erosion of land and people at the end of the thirties was so intense as to make the Wallace solution of the ever-normal granary seem of doubtful conviction, while a tacked-on defense "epilogue" partook of the pathos of another documentary of the period which, in a classic attempt to recapture timeliness, said in its commentary: "Now that we are at war, hospitalization of unmarried mothers is more important than ever." Could such a film accomplish anything if it were released; might it not actually do harm? While the Department officials pondered, the Japanese struck at Pearl Harbor. That was that. *The Land* was permitted a gala *première* at the Museum of Modern Art early in 1942, but further showings were prohibited.

Flaherty always continued to hope that *The Land* would one day find its audience. In the postwar world that has been, if anything, less possible than during wartime. Agricultural employment continues high, and, despite disturbing warnings from those who should know, our policy continues to be to plant every inch

141

of land in order to feed our increased population, plus as much of the rest of the world as may be. Viewed against the background of our current thinking and doing, *The Land* seems fantastically out of the argument, and today it is almost a forgotten film.

Even in its day, its survey of the problems of the land was little to the liking of the agriculture experts or of the devotees of the "sociological" documentary. They found both its statement and its solution personal, naïve, "romantic." Personal *The Land* undoubtedly is, it being beyond Flaherty to be impersonal. He felt involved in the tragic problem, and the solution through an imaginative use of machines was one in which he truly believed. A disinterested critic, Siegfried Kracauer, seems to have revealed better than anyone how closely this apparently uncharacteristic film approached the general Flaherty view of things:

The weak sides of this film are too obvious to dwell upon. Its plot lacks precision and fails to get hold of the very problems it attacks . . . Perhaps Flaherty has worked too long on his film; this would be an explanation for motifs abandoned on the way and for the incoherence of the different parts.

But all these deficiencies are not weighty enough to injure the true merits of *The Land:* its deep honesty and the beauty of its pictures. Indeed, the whole is impregnated with a sincerity that cannot but impress. Flaherty may be naïve; in his naïveté, however, he really says what he feels and avoids making hasty conclusions. And if he does not always come to grips with the problems he wants to expose, *he proceeds, nevertheless, with an instinct so infallible as not to endanger future solutions*. It is important that his own voice sounds throughout the film; this voice has the power of convincing and efficaciously bolsters the content of the pictures.

The secret of these pictures is to include *time*. They resemble fragments of a lost epic song that celebrated the immense life of the land; nothing is omitted, and each episode is full of significance. Among them that with the old Negro slowly wiping and then ringing the bell belongs to the unforgettable scenes on the screen.

It is as "fragments of a lost epic song" that *The Land* appears today to those film connoisseurs who value it as an example of Flaherty's great eye and beautiful craftsmanship. That is perhaps not all, or not enough. The loss of the soil goes on, whether we choose to recognize it at the moment or not. And this outcry against the loss of the land, which Flaherty loved as he loved all the elements of life, may yet seem to us a patriarchal warning.

PART SIX

Louisiana Story

In THE SPRING of 1942 Frank Capra, then at the head of the War Department film division, engaged Flaherty to make a camera survey of war production for use as a regular newsreel for the armed forces to be called *The State of the Nation*. Probably this project was doomed from the start. The rapid shooting necessary for weekly release ran counter to Flaherty's instincts and training; picture-making under military supervision proved more irksome even than Hollywood's interference; and, above all, the Hollywood-trained cutters who constituted Capra's army editing staff were bewildered by the material Flaherty sent in from the field, since it failed to obey the "laws" of newsreel editing. Beset by problems, Capra found it easiest to jettison this one. Flaherty's services were no longer required for army film-making. Nor were other wartime government agencies able to see what his talent could lend to their sometimes pedestrian propagandist activities. The young men who staffed them may not have been particularly eager to put their own work in competition with that of this veteran, and the whisper was heard that Flaherty belonged to the past — a glorious past, indeed, but not one that fitted a man for the making of "modern" documentaries. One authority went so far as to say, "Flaherty? Why, it would be like asking an old-time carriage maker to manufacture a Cadillac."

There were, however, those who *could* "see" Flaherty in relation to the contemporary scene. The Standard Oil Company, casting about for some one who could serve their public relations aims, happened upon the fact that *Nanook of the North,* sponsored by a commercial firm, had been shown all over the world and was hailed as a classic with no complaint from anyone that its finances might be tainted. The result was an extraordinary contract, by which Standard Oil provided complete finance for Flaherty's next film but left him its sole owner, with no obligation to repay the negative cost and with distribution rights entirely in his hands.

Moreover, in the grand tradition of Ivy Lee, Standard Oil stipulated that no mention of its sponsorship of the film should appear in the screen credits.

What followed is a remarkable example of the working methods the Flahertys developed over a period of thirty years. Their mandate was to discover and disclose to the public the drama, and even the heroism, involved in taking oil from the earth, just as they had revealed the drama and heroism of staying alive in the North and on Aran.

In the course of my luncheons with the Standard Oil people they managed to communicate to me some of the excitement and fascination that surrounds the oil business. The upshot of it was that I agreed to spend three months finding out whether I thought I could make an interesting picture about oil.

Mrs. Flaherty and I set out in our car for the Southwest. We drove thousands of miles. We visited boom towns and ghost towns and listened to the tales spun by old-timers. We found limitless plains, dotted with derricks.

But we kept reminding ourselves that even in westerns, horses galloped. In the oil country, the derricks stand straight and rigid against the sky. Nothing moved. We couldn't get it out of our minds that the real drama of oil was taking place deep in the earth at that very moment, concealed from the eye of the camera.

At length we came to the bayou country of Louisiana. We were enchanted by the gentle, gay, and picturesque people of French descent who inhabit this little known section of the United States;

a people who have managed to preserve the individual flavour of their culture. We were delighted with their customs, their superstitions, their folk-tales of werewolves and mermaids, handed down from generation to generation. But we weren't getting any closer to a film about oil.

Then one day we stopped the car for lunch near the edge of a bayou. Suddenly over the heads of the marsh grass, an oil derrick came into our view. It was moving up the bayou, towed by a launch. In motion, this familiar structure suddenly became poetry, its slim lines rising clean and taut above the unending flatness of the marshes.

I looked at Frances. She looked at me. We knew then we had our picture.

Almost immediately a story began to take shape in our minds. It was a story built around that derrick which moved so silently, so majestically into the wilderness; probed for oil beneath the watery ooze, and then moved on again, leaving the land as untouched as before it came.

The story almost wrote itself. We shot it up to New York and got an okay from Standard's board of directors. Only at that point did we make a definite deal to go ahead with the film.

Meanwhile, we had moved to Abbeville, Louisiana, in the heart of the bayou country. We rented a lovely old house on a back street where we set up field headquarters with a small staff: Frances and myself, Ricky Leacock, our cameraman, Helen van Dongen, associate producer and editor; later our daughter Barbara, who had come from her home in India during the war, joined us for a while. There we all lived together for nearly two years.

We converted a huge closet into a dark room and the front porch into a sitting room, where Helen sat, day after day, with the growing reels of film, while the rest of us were out shooting.

At night our little family had its meals together, and sometimes we played cards or had some music. Mostly, though, like all filmmakers we spent our evenings discussing the story, screening the day's rushes, or cutting, cutting, cutting some more. My definition of a film is "the longest distance between two points," and once you're into it, you eat it and sleep it.

For our hero, we dreamed up a half-wild Cajun boy of the

woods and bayous. To personalize the theme of the impact of industry, we developed the character of an oil driller who would become a friend of the boy, eventually overcoming his shyness and reticence. Then came the difficult business of casting. I spend perhaps more time on this aspect of picture-making than any other, for I believe that the secret of success in making this type of film lies in finding the right people.

We broke up into parties and combed the countryside for the types we were seeking, taking literally hundreds of photographs of people.

Almost at once we ran into Lionel Le Blanc, who was a natural both in manner and looks to play the old trapper who was to be the father of our boy-hero.

Mrs. Flaherty and Rickey Leacock heard about a promising boy in a remote parish and decided to drive over and have a look at him. On the way, they stopped in at a cabin to ask directions and there, staring at them from a photograph on top of the radio, was the face of Joseph Boudreaux, the boy who plays the lead in *Louisiana Story*. But Joseph had gone to the nearest town for an ice cream cone, walking the twelve miles barefoot. My wife and Rickey immediately got in the car and went to look for him, afraid to get too excited until they had run the necessary tests. They found him resting on a curbstone, shot their shots, and hurried home.

We all held our breath. But in the tests he looked just as appealing as he had in the photograph on the radio. We had our boy.

In the meantime, we were coming to the conclusion that Frank Hardy, a Texan who had grown up in the oil fields, and who was working locally on a nearby rig, was just right for the role of the oil driller. But Frank was so shy that speaking his lines was almost a physical pain. Still, there was something engaging about his shyness, and as he got used to the idea, he developed into a real actor.

We didn't try to "cast" the other drillers. We just took over the crew of Humble Petite Anse No. 1, put at our disposal by Humble Oil and Refining Company, a Standard affiliate.

We had established a relationship between our boy and the men of the huge derrick that had moved onto his father's land to probe

150

for oil beneath the waters of the bayou. Now we had to show the dangers, as well as the gamble, involved in drilling for oil in this way. In the beginning the derrick crew, although coolly courteous, obviously regarded our presence as an interruption of their work. But as time went on, and they saw how we were trying to catch the drama of their own lives, they caught the fever of motion picture making and took a fascinated interest in all our activity.

We worked day after day, shooting reams of stuff. But somehow we never could seem to make that pesky derrick come alive. We could not recapture that exhilaration we had felt when we first saw it slowly moving up the bayou.

Then we hit on it. At night! That's when it was alive!

At night, with the derrick lights dancing and flickering on the dark surface of the water, the excitement that is the very essence of drilling for oil became visual. So we threw our daytime footage into the ashcan and started in all over again to shoot our drilling scenes against a night background.

So far so good. But to make an unusual picture, we needed something out of the ordinary, something which does not occur in the usual run of events. But major disturbances seldom happen in the scientific, carefully controlled activity that is the modern oil business. Just the same, we would have to show some sort of catastrophe if we were to make our audiences see that bringing oil from the earth involves constant hazard as well as the chance that the oil man's labors will go for nothing.

I've been lucky in my motion pictures. But I believe in making your luck, too. I arranged with one of the state conservation department officers and with the tool pushers of the Humble Company, who get around a lot, that if anything were to go wrong anywhere within reach, they were to let me know immediately.

For weeks nothing happened. Then about two o'clock one morning we got the phone call. A well at Atchafalaya Bay about sixty miles away had a gas blow. We were dressed and aboard our cabin cruiser in record time. I was so excited, as we sped along through the night, that I knocked over an oil lantern and nearly burnt the boat out from under us. But we got the fire out and reached the well about 10 A.M. She was still spouting gas, water, and mud.

151

With the temerity born of ignorance, we clambered aboard and began to shoot. We got up on the upper floor of the derrick, and, shooting from there, got some magnificent footage looking right down into the spouting gas.

Finally one of the rig bosses came up and looked curiously at the camera. When he saw its electric motor, his hair stood straight on end. "For God's sake, get out of here with those cameras," he shouted over the noise of the gas.

When we were at a safe distance from the derrick, he explained more calmly that if the motor on our camera had generated a spark, with all that gas floating in the air we would have blown up the countryside for three miles around. We sat down hard when we heard that one. But we had our footage!

We hadn't yet given much thought to what was to prove our biggest headache. That was making the sound track on our drilling sequences. Although the spectator would not realize it, there are seven separate sound tracks running through the drilling scenes. Each sound had to be sorted out from the others and recorded separately, for if they are recorded all together every sound has a tendency to interfere with each of the others.

From the very first we had been fascinated with the sound a derrick makes. The mighty clash and ring of the steel pipe, the clatter of the block and the cables, with the steady throb of the engines running underneath it all, had the qualities of a great symphony. This sound proved to be an inspiration to Virgil Thomson, too, when he came to write the music for the film.

We tried for days to sort out the various sounds without success. Finally we built a shanty on the bank to house our recording equipment, and strung our microphones at every conceivable point. All night we would sit there, hoping that if we stayed with it long enough we would get the particular sound we wanted without interference. Sometimes the drilling operation had to be shut down entirely. But after weeks of heartache, we got it.

Our last job was to gather what we call "wild sound," that is, the noises such as animal and bird cries, the sound of water lapping, etc., to match the scenes which had to be shot without sound. We had little trouble with the animal noises. We had but to ap-

"The derrick, moving so silently, so majestically into the wilderness"

"A lovely old house on a back street where we set up field headquarters"

Leacock, Helen van Dongen, Flaherty, Joseph, Frances Flaherty

"Like all film-makers, we spent our evenings discussing the story, and screening the day's rushes"

Flaherty, Joseph Boudreaux, unidentified man, Helen van Dongen (editor), Frances Flaherty, Richard Leacock (cameraman)

"A half-wild Cajun boy of the woods and bayous"

"Here in the bayou we built our pontoons, set up our cameras — and waited. We had a general notion of what this part of the story would be like, but we wanted to get ideas by watching the creatures of this watery wilderness in action. Day after day we sat there in the broiling sun, shooting everything we saw"

"Here is the sequence as we finally developed it. Our boy — Alexander
Napoleon Ulysses Latour — is fishing in the bayou with his pet raccoon,
Jo-Jo. He sees something on the bank and goes to investigate. Left alone,
Jo-Jo breaks his leash and slips off into the water. An alligator spies the
coon and starts after him"

"Jo-Jo swims for dear life!"

"Meanwhile, Alexander has made a discovery — an alligator's nest! The eggs are just hatching. He picks up the baby 'gators. He turns around — not a moment too soon — for — "

"*MAMA* has come back!"

"He just makes it out of her reach. Her lunge is as swift as a panther's"

"When Alexander returns to his boat, Jo-Jo is gone! Disconsolately he searches the woods, hoping that the coon has wandered off. But in his heart he is sure the big alligator got him"

"Alexander prepares his revenge — a wicked hook baited with beefsteak"

"The 'gator takes the bait, and the tug of war begins"

"Slowly the alligator's strength begins to tell. Alexander's feet slide down
the bank — toward the water"

"Fortunately his father has become worried and gone in search of him, and arrives just in time to save him from being pulled under"

"So the alligator got away — this time. But with his father's help, Alexander does succeed in trapping him, and here is the trophy to prove it. Of course Jo-Jo wasn't eaten by the alligator — he got away safe and sound, and rejoins his master at the end of the picture"

proach the alligator and he emitted his terrifying sound like the hiss of escaping steam.

The first part of the film was to be the story of a Cajun boy's life in the swamps and bayous of backwoods Louisiana, hunting and fishing with his pet raccoon, Jo-Jo. Now for choosing the location. Here Colonel Ned McIlhenny, internationally known explorer and sportsman, was a godsend to us. His fantastic estate, Avery Island, is one of the show places of the south with its well-stocked wildlife preserve. He gave us free access to the place and it was here that we recruited a number of our animal actors, including that magnificent, hard-breathing "heavy," the alligator.

Here in the middle of the bayou we built pontoons, set up our cameras — and waited.

We had a general notion of what this part of the story would be like, but we wanted to get ideas by watching the creatures of this watery wilderness in action. Day after day we sat there in the broiling sun, watching them, shooting everything we saw. Of them all, decidedly the most impressive was the alligator.

We saw a baby aigret, too young to fly, trapped on a snag of driftwood. An alligator spotted it and swam over to collect the tempting morsel. The aigret stood still, paralyzed with fright. Unless we intervened, he seemed doomed. But the aigret escaped! The driftwood was too light to bear the 'gator's weight.

Here is the sequence as we finally developed it. Our boy — Alexander Napoleon Ulysses Latour is his name — is fishing in the bayou with his pet raccoon.

He sees something on the bank which attracts his attention and he goes to investigate, leaving his coon tethered in the boat.

The coon, left alone, breaks his leash and slips off into the water.

An alligator — the one that missed the baby aigret — spies the coon and starts after him. Jo-Jo swims for dear life!

Meanwhile, Alexander has made a discovery — an alligator's nest! The eggs are just hatching. He picks up the baby 'gators.

He turns around — not a moment too soon. Mama has come back!

He just makes it out of reach — her lunge is as swift as a panther's.

153

When Alexander returns to his boat, Jo-Jo is gone! Disconsolately he searches the woods, hoping against hope that the coon has wandered off. But in his heart he is sure that the big alligator got him.

Alexander prepares his revenge — a wicked hook baited with beefsteak.

The 'gator approaches the bait — and takes it. Then the tug of war begins.

Slowly the alligator's strength begins to tell. Alexander's feet slide down the bank — toward the water.

Fortunately his father had become worried and had gone in search of him.

And arrived just in time to save him from being pulled under.

So the alligator got away — this time. But with his father's help, Alexander did succeed in trapping him, and here is the trophy to prove it. Of course Jo-Jo wasn't eaten by the alligator — he got away safe and sound, and re-joins his master at the end of the picture.

You might think the alligator sequence would be the climax of our picture, but it was only an introductory highlight. The real climax was the oil drilling sequence — the complicated marvel of driving thousands of feet of steel tubing miles into the bowels of the earth where the oil is waiting, buried deep in the strata of the Carboniferous Era. No still picture can render the drama of this process, nor the magnificent courage and skill of the men who drill for oil. They get just as excited over bringing in a well as though it were a once-in-a-lifetime event instead of routine they follow day after day and year after year.

Our story, you know, ends with the capping of the well with a "Christmas Tree" — a sort of spigot which can be turned off and on at will, and to which pipelines are attached. Alexander, whose family has benefited from the leasing of the land by the oil company, sits on the Christmas tree and waves good-bye to his friends the drillers as the huge derrick is towed off to another bayou, another gamble for oil.

PART SEVEN

The World of Robert Flaherty

A FEW MONTHS before he died, I was talking to Bob Flaherty in his suite at the Hotel Chelsea on 23rd Street in New York. The shabby old rooms were stacked with the loot of years of travel. Sunshine filtered in through dusty windows on cameras and tripods lined against the wall. Stills from the films were propped up on the mantelpiece for me to look at. On the coffee-stained work table was a pile of messages from passers-through New York who wanted to give him a hail. He had lived there six years, on and off, but it all looked like a camp that might be struck at dawn. As ever, he was poised for flight.

Where to, this time? He paced the room as I quizzed him on future film plans about which he was vague. I was persistent; I wanted to know exactly what he saw ahead of him. Suddenly he sat down and looked at me and said, "Well, say what you will, there's one thing they can't take away from us, the way we've lived these thirty years."

I wasn't up to replying to that autumnal remark, but I have thought long thoughts about it ever since. It may be that he foresaw what was about to happen, and was balancing out profit and loss. More likely he was reminding himself, as he periodically did, what, when all was said and done, he was really after.

He had need of such reminder, three-and-a-half years after the release of *Louisiana Story*. The picture was one of his successes. The press, especially the picture magazines, had a field-day with it; everybody agreed that it was great, and its maker greater still;

157

he was famous all over again. In Europe, especially, they loved the film, and the State Department conceived the bright idea of sending Flaherty to Germany as a sort of ambassador of good will. Here, they reasoned, was an American creative figure of whom the right sort of symbol could be made, a figure nobody could identify with the alleged vulgarities of American industrial civilization, and who certainly could not be confused with high finance. He stood for art for art's sake and nothing else but and, as such, would be the perfect antidote to certain unjust but widely held notions about life in the United States.

The calculation proved correct. The Germans knew all about Robert Flaherty and what he stood for. His tour of the American zone was one of the positive achievements of the State Department. True, he said very little about American know-how, free enterprise, and so forth. He said, indeed, very little at all since he knew no German and had to speak through a translator. This proved to be no barrier to his achieving the desired effect. The Germans in any case did not want to hear from him about America, they wanted to hear about his life and travels — to shut out the cold gray world of their defeat and go with him vicariously to Samoa and India and the Louisiana bayous.

Probably the question that had to be translated to him most often was, "What will your next film be?" I don't know what was translated back by way of reply. Nor do I know what he answered to the same question when it was put to him by André Gide, Pablo Picasso, and the other notables who made much of him in Paris. In London, though there too there was much homage, the question probably didn't arise. The British, among whom he had tried to make films, already knew the answer. What was salient in all this was that none of those who asked the question so enthusiastically had any very feasible suggestion to make as to what the next film might be and, more to the purpose, how he might go about making it. So, after a nostalgic visit to Aran, where he stayed a few nights in the cottage he owned there, renewed old acquaint-ances and burned some old film, he sailed back to New York.

Here perhaps the success of his tour and the honors heaped upon him might have tangible results. There were none. World-famous and world-loved, his standing in his own profession was nil. You might suppose that a master film director who would work for a salary normally paid an assistant would be in great demand, but that is not the way of things in the film world. There, they distrust people who put a low price on themselves, especially if it is suspected that the lowness of the price is a bargaining point in return for a free hand with the film. Much better to ask the moon and then shoot the script they give you, word for word. After the West Coast première of *Louisiana Story,* Charlie Chap-lin, Jean Renoir, and Dudley Nichols had wired Flaherty: DO THIS AGAIN AND YOU WILL BE IMMORTAL, AND EXCOMMUNICATED FROM HOLLYWOOD, WHICH IS A GOOD FATE. The praise of these eminent and entrenched Californians had a sting in its tail. For Flaherty was *already* excommunicated from Hollywood, had been for long years, and non-professional sponsorship was increasingly difficult to find, even after *Louisiana Story,* even after Europe.

Of course, the State Department was pleased with his German successes, and there was talk of a film for the Division of Motion Pictures, which is the branch of State charged with making films to project American life before the world. It was thought that Flaherty might well make a film of Hawaii and its melting pot of races, where Polynesians and Caucasians and Mongolians live together amicably under the American flag. It would, of course, have to be a small film and very inexpensive, and it would have to be carefully planned. It would have to be talked over. It was talked over for going onto two years. It was still being talked over when Flaherty died.

He had occupied himself in the meantime with several experi-ments with films about painting, and with a three-dimensional film camera which Mike Todd and Lowell Thomas were preparing to exploit. But his real hopes had been pinned on the Hawaiian film, or one like it. His death, still hoping, left those of us who knew him with the confounding thought that this man who had been deemed worthy to represent his country abroad, on the record of his achievement in the most characteristically American art, could find no agency, public or private, willing to back him in applying that art in the service of the United States.

I leave the patriotic reader to ponder the paradox. From where I sit, it looks like a plain case of waste of natural resources, and the feeling is difficult to suppress that someone should be brought to book for it. At the same time, suspicion occurs that the culprit is composite and includes all of us. If guilt there is, it can't be atomized into blaming Hollywood for its commercialism, government agencies for their timidity, or educational institutions for their blindness to a magical instrument of education which he forged and offered to put into their hands. Hollywood is supposed to be commercial, government agencies are wise to be timid, and conservatism, shall we say, is generally considered a virtue in academic circles. But something is lacking from the make-up of a society which gives a man the accolade of genius and then makes it all but impossible for him to do the work he was born to do.

However that may be, the problem is ours, not his. He did not consider that anyone had a duty to help him make films. True, he fathered the documentary film, whose later exponents sought subsidy on the ground that what they were doing was in the public interest and therefore should not be forced to compete in the market place. All this he viewed benevolently, and even tried his hand at it with *The Land*. But he did not really think that the kind of film he wanted to make had its most direct bearing in the fields of politics, sociology, or even education in the formal sense. Perhaps the movies could serve us in these immediate concerns, but not his kind of film. He wanted his kind of film to shift our at-

Robert Flaherty, 1928

Moana, 1925

Robert Flaherty Directing

Man of Aran, 1933

Louisiana Story, 1946

Flaherty, 1951

The Flahertys in Europe, 1949

tention from what was under our noses to a larger vision of the
world.

His vision of the world was simple, but hard to communicate
because it came out of experiences from which most of us are cut
off. Inherent gifts, and a boyhood spent face to face with nature,
prepared him for the event which crystallized his outlook, his life
with the Eskimos. That experience has been eloquently described
by the Frenchman Gontran de Poncins, one of the few men who
have, like Flaherty, lived with the Eskimos by choice and as one of
them. At the end of his book, *Kabloona,* de Poncins says:

> . . . I thought of the months on the trail, of the hardships
> and even miseries I had endured, and of a sudden I began to miss
> them with an intensity which amazed me and which, since then,
> has never left me. For one does miss these trials, indeed, more than
> anything else. One remembers them without remembering what
> they made of one. Man thinks of the thing rather than the idea.
> The hospital patient, once cured, remembers less his recovery than
> the bed of pain on which he lay; and for my part I have never
> yearned with as much tenderness for anything as for the polar
> winter and those transient shelters in the snows.
>
> God knows we were poor enough. Our poverty was total. We
> possessed nothing; not even the snow was our own. As a bird
> carries off a twig with which to make its nest, then leaves that bor-
> rowed twig once the season has passed, so we cut and trimmed
> our borrowed snow and left it to return to the common lot . . .
> But there was a cheer and a contentment in our existence which I
> continue to muse upon and cannot altogether explain to myself.
> Was it because infinite poverty lent infinite price to the least ob-
> ject? There was more to it than this . . . Within me had lain
> potentialities for moral serenity and I had not known it. Storm and
> danger had been my salvation, and without them my spirit should
> have dropped heedlessly off to sleep in my flesh. There on that
> Arctic tundra I had reconstructed myself from within. Up through
> the lined and frozen layers of skin on my face, my true visage had
> begun to emerge, the visage that God had meant all men to show

to one another; and that visage all the blizzards, all the adversity in the world could not decompose.

. . . I cannot pretend of course to lend to the Eskimos these thoughts I now express. The poverty that was my salvation had from the beginning of time been theirs, and so long as they were uncontaminated they lived in obedience to the high code that it commanded. But I was rediscovering that code. I was rounding out the cycle of life in my return to a point on that cycle which the Eskimos had never left. Those men about whom I knew properly nothing at all, those beings of another race separated from me by thousands of years of the evolution of my kind, had stood shoulder to shoulder with me in the blizzard. With my friends Outside there had always been differences, we had always remained personalities, individuals. Here, after the first few weeks of my probation, none of this existed; the contact was direct, devoid of the detours of personality. Day after day a wind would rise, a sign of danger would appear in the air, and we would respond together, each forgetting himself and striving in the common cause. Outside, it wanted war and flood to give man this sense of brotherhood; here it was a commonplace of life. And if I write this now, and am moved by the memory of it, the reason is that these were the only moments of my life when I was describable not as a Frenchman, not as an individual product of heritage, place, environment, but as nothing other than, simply, a man.

These are the words of a man to whom this experience came late. It came to Flaherty in the morning of his life and was therefore harder for him to articulate, because it was habitual with him. But it was the mainspring of his life and film-making. Everywhere he went he looked for this spirit in men, and always found it somehow — even in the sun-blessed Polynesians, even in the destroyed lives broken down by the roadside of depression America. The Flaherty school of film-making was once dubbed "Romantic Naturalism" by the critics, as if he were a Rousseau primitivist trying to recapture some lost and perhaps imaginary Eden. He was not. He was a realist of mankind. He wanted to show us

162

situations which put men to the test, and how they met the test. It was easier to show this in primitive settings, because there the test was the obvious one of the struggle to stay alive. But I would be willing to bet that his one film of city life, the unfinished *Twenty-Four Dollar Island,* would have been no different in its values and intentions from any of his other films. He judged men everywhere in the same way, by the way they met the tests they were put to, whatever the tests were. What you had to learn to understand about him, and it took time, was that his standards were always basic and were unaffected by the labels we ordinarily use as guideposts in judging people. You wouldn't, for example, expect him to admire a movie star, and it was surprising to learn that he admired so effulgent a star as Gloria Swanson. His explanation made everything clear: "Gloria has courage."

His behavior in cities, where alone I knew him, always seemed to me to be pretty much the way he must have behaved in Ungava or any other wild place. Gontran de Poncins, describing an Eskimo visit to his hut, says: "The visit lasted exactly the length of time required to clean me out of provisions; for it is again a matter of Eskimo etiquette that nothing be left unconsumed." In the same way, the host holds nothing back; in the North, men share all they have. Anyone who saw him holding forth at the Coffee House Club in New York or elsewhere saw this code in action. Being served at his table was as if you took the food as a gift from his hands, you must always have another drink, just one, and above all things you mustn't go home. In his presence you weren't allowed to pay for so much as a postage stamp. A checkbook was a means of facilitating the diffusion of money, a savings account was nonexistent. In the North, men share all they have.

He felt instinctively that everything created by man belonged to everybody, a vast pool on which all were free to draw. And he felt that creation was man's principal business. It surprised those who thought of him as a primitivist when he filled *The Land* and

163

Louisiana Story with visual poems to machinery, but it should not have surprised them. He loved all making and doing, and understood it, which is why he could make any piece of craftsmanship, from basket-weaving to oil-drilling, come alive dramatically on the screen, while others made of the same processes only a perfunctory description. You could always enlist his interest in anything which had to do with invention, with devising, with creation, and it did not matter whether it was great or small. Once when I came to see him he put into my hands a queer little gadget. I asked what it was for. "It threads a needle!" he said gleefully.

Sharing and making and liking are the qualities you think of when he comes to mind. He liked nearly everything. He wanted everything that breathed to have its place in the sun, and this came from the depths of him, whatever the ironies of its surface manifestations. Men who live as Bob Flaherty lived, explorers, adventurers, "men of action," commonly have a keen and well-developed hunting instinct. It was lacking in him. He was not sentimental about wild creatures; he knew they preyed on one another as we prey on them. But so far as I know he never killed except for food. I can't honestly say I know exactly why; the two or three times that I discussed the subject with him, he had no generalities to offer, he just said he didn't like it. His wife, in one of her books, felt called upon to explain that "shooting," when mentioned by the Flahertys, always meant shooting with the camera, never with guns.

I have said very little about the kind of "shooting" he did do. As far as I can make it so, this is a book about the man and the life he led, the "thirty years they can't take away from us," and not about the films as such. But this much should be said: his art grew directly out of his character. He was the first film director to understand that the eye of the camera does not behave like the human eye, which selects from a field of vision only what interests its owner. The camera's eye unselectively records every-

164

thing before it. Most film-makers try to force the camera to "see" what they have already determined will be there to see. A sense of wonder and delight in all things under the sun made Robert Flaherty trust the camera before himself. He wanted what the camera's eye could show him that his own eye could not see. Because of this, he shot everything, and only afterward, in the projection room, did he really "make" his films, looking at all he had photographed again and again until the underlying pattern emerged for him. His was first of all an art of observation and afterward of selection.

The principle of selection was simple. He tried to show in his films, what he embodied so fully in his own person, "the visage that God had meant all men to show to one another."

Date Due